For:- Kenneth Moynihan.

With Best Wishes.

[signature]

Editor
Justin Nelson

ISBN 1 900913 02 X
ISBN 1 900913 03 8

Printed by;
Kilkenny People Printing,
Purcellsinch Industrial Estate,
Kilkenny.

A CIP catalogue record for this book is available from the British Library.

First Published July 1997.
Reprinted October 1997.
Reprinted September 1998.
Reprinted January 2002.
Publisher; © Justin Nelson Productions Ltd., 151 Foxrock Park, Dublin 18.

MICHAEL COLLINS

The Final Days

Justin Nelson

Hang Up Your Brightest Colours

"How could a born soldier die better than at the victorious end of a good fight, falling to the shot of another Irishman, – a damned fool, but all the same an Irishman who thought he was fighting for Ireland – 'a Roman to a Roman'?

I met Michael for the first and last time on Saturday last, and am very glad I did. I rejoice in his memory and will not be so disloyal to it as to snivel over his valiant death.

So tear up your mourning and hang up your brightest colours in his honour; and let us all praise God that he had not to die in a snuffy bed of a trumpery cough, weakened by age, and saddened by the disappointments that would have attended his work had he lived".

George Bernard Shaw *in a letter to Collins' sister Hannie*

CONTENTS

PREFACE

It is now 80 years since the Civil War and the tragic death of General Michael Collins. I have included in this book photos and articles published around the time of his death.

Of particular interest will be the reprints from the "Souvenir Album of the Dublin Fighting 1922". This booklet was published some time after July 12th. 1922, but as it was out of date within a matter of weeks following the deaths of both Griffith and Collins, it may never have been circulated. In addition the contemporary account of the 1916 Rising as published in "The Sinn Fein Revolt Illustrated" and "The Rebellion in Dublin" makes interesting reading now more than 80 years later. I have also reprinted extracts from the Arthur Griffith / Michael Collins Memorial booklet published soon afterwards.

For the first time too a member of the Collins family agreed to have a comprehensive account of the period published giving the family version of this dramatic period. For this, and for making available a selection of photographs and documents, some of which had never been published, I will be forever grateful to the General's nephew, another Michael Collins who has sadly died since the publication of the early editions of this book. The fact that he was delighted with the way the publication turned out in book form gives me great satisfaction, and I dedicate this fourth printing to his memory. May he rest in peace with his famous uncle.

Gone from us too is a dear friend James O'Callaghan, who like myself, has had a life-long interest in photography. It was he who first whetted my enthusiasm for this project when he gave me his unique collection of historic negatives from the period. An example is his picture of the burning of the Customs house which he photographed on 25th. May 1921, together with negatives of Arthur Griffith's funeral. On page 11 we see the newly appointed Commander-in-Chief along side Richard Mulcahy at the Griffith funeral, just six days before his own death at Beal na Blath, and the subsequent photos of Collins' own funeral from his collection are now published for the first time.

I must also thank RTE for the use of material from its archives, Ben Klaasen, Eileen Larkin, Gerry O Donovan and my former TV colleague, the late Brendan O'Reilly, who gave me access to their private collections, Examiner Publications who so readily gave me permission to reprint material from the Cork Examiner supplement "The Big Fellow" as well as the authors concerned.

Copies from the early editions of this book have gone to the four corners of the world through contacts via the internet, and it is mainly for these international Collins fans that I am printing this fourth edition. Surely when Michael Collins worked as a boy clerk in the London Post Office he could never have imagined the concept of the World Wide Web or that he himself would one day be the subject of so many web pages on the Internet.

Finally my thanks to all the photographers who in many cases risked their lives to provide the visual memory of this dramatic period of our history for future generations to treasure.

Justin Nelson. Editor.

For my parents Peter and Tess
whose politics I have never known

LET US BURY THE DEAD PAST

"Many of you were on opposite sides. Let us leave it at that. Each of us, like I did myself, believed in the correctness of our choice.

Let us end all the futile recriminations of an event which happened so many years ago and which divided brother against brother and neighbour against neighbour. Here at this monument erected to commemorate for all time the greatness of the contribution made by Michael Collins in our struggle for freedom, let us bury the dead past of dissensions.

He, who we knew hated the civil war and all its sad consequences, would have us all do so.

Michael Collins would be the first to deny any suggestion that he alone won this dour struggle. He realised that this struggle was one of teamwork and that other leaders of that period played their part in the victory.

However it can be said with certainty that no man inside Ireland or outside it, contributed more than Michael Collins to the fight for Irish Independence".

GENERAL TOM BARRY'S ADDRESS AT THE UNVEILING OF A MEMORIAL TO MICHAEL COLLINS AT SAM'S CROSS IN AUGUST 1965.

General Tom Barry with Mr. Michael Collins, nephew of General Collins at the memorial at Sam's Cross.

MICHAEL COLLINS REMEMBERED

The scene at Beal na mBláth on Sunday 24th. August 1997 when thousands attended the Collins commemoration Ceremony marking the 75th. anniversary of his death at this spot on a quiet roadside in his native West Cork.

On August 16th, 1922 Michael Collins and Richard Mulcahy led the army officers in Arthur Griffith's funeral cortege.
Six days later General Collins would be shot dead.

Ministers at the funeral of General Collins. Left to right – E. Duggan, Eoin Mac Neill, J.J. Walsh, W.T. Cosgrave, P. Hogan, Ernest Blythe, Desmond Fitzgerald, ____, Joe McGrath, ____.

Michael Collins has had many biographers down the years, but this is the first comprehensive account giving the Collins family side of the story ever published.

His nephew, - also christened Michael Collins, has a further singular connection which makes his memories unique. His mother was none other than the legendary Nancy O'Brien who was entrusted with decoding messages from the British, and which she secretly smuggled out to General Collins with devastating effect.

This account is adapted by the Editor from a talk given by Michael Collins to the Clonmel Historical Society in April '97.

MY UNCLE

By Michael Collins

Michael Collins was born in "Woodfield" near Sam's Cross, Clonakilty, West Cork. The Collins family were evicted from their homes in Limerick in the latter part of the 17th Century. They were troublesome even then, and causing so many problems that the decision of the Magistrate was to banish this unruly and troublesome clan to the nether-most regions of the King's Realm,- known as West Cork, where they and their descendants would never again cause any difficulty to his Majesty's liege men and women. In this, they succeeded for a few hundred years, but after this lapse, Michael Collins made up for it!.

Collins' father, that is my grandfather, was almost 60 years when he married, for he had to wait, as was normal in those days, until my great grandfather had died. He then took the land which was occupied by three brothers, Maurice, Thomas, and himself

The young Michael Collins with his mother Mary Anne, his grandmother, sister and brother Johnnie, father of the writer.

Michael John Collins. He married Mary Anne O' Brien of Sam's Cross who was 34 years younger than him. They had a most wonderful marriage, from which was born eight children, five girls and three boys. Early in 1877 their first child Margaret was born, to be followed by Johnny, (my father), Johanna (called Hannie), Mary, Helena (who later became a Nun), Patrick, Kathleen and finally Michael.

Grandfather Michael Collins and Mary Anne O'Brien could speak Greek and Latin fluently and also Irish, which they learned from the hedge schoolmasters at the time. Though there was a very large gap in years between them, their's was a very close and fruitful relationship.

Michael Collins was the youngest of the family of eight and was born in Woodfield on the 16th of October, 1890.

He had a reverence from the time he was a very small boy for elderly people, and he had not an unusual but unique relationship with his father for the few years they shared together. My grandfather had a particular habit of once a week devoting twenty entire minutes to each of his children separately.

My father, Johnny, the eldest in the family, absorbed the knowledge of agriculture, horticulture and mariculture imparted to him by his father. Hannie, the eldest of the girls, absorbed his extraordinary knowledge of English literature, while Helena who later became a nun knew every constellation in the sky from her father's teaching. She recalled to me how clearly he said to her one day when one of the comets was passing, -

"I haven't had much time in my busy life, Helena, to get down on my knees and pray, - but when I'm out here like I am to-night and see the majesty of the Heavens I tell Him 'I believe You made it, and I believe also that I am a tiny subject of Yours". "You can do a lot of praying, Helena" he said "but you won't get much closer to God than when you are under the creation of the stars".

Michael, at that young age of four, heard the poems of Kickham and Davis from this old man who was his father. My grandfather, Michael John Collins, had in his library every single work of Shakespeare, and the works of Thomas Hardy, and Sir Peter Barrie. He was an insatiable reader and to each of the children in turn he imparted his philosophy of life.

"I haven't been over burdened with the wealth of this life, but I will give you three things which I hope will always stand to you in life, – namely a strong faith, a work ethic, and a love of education, for as you educate yourselves, you will, if it is within your potential, build yourselves into men and women who think for themselves."

(Above) Michael's mother on left, his sister Mary and grandmother.

(Below) They are joined by sisters Margaret and Katie with brothers Pat and Johnnie outside the family home at Lisavaird near Clonakilty, Co. Cork.

"I will impart to you the love of my country which is one of my greatest gifts". This was not the "pint inspired" love of Ireland. This was an old man giving to his children his love of the culture, of the heritage, of the real Irish tradition, the music of Ireland and the writings of men like Charles Kickham and Davis.

My grandfather, and Michael's father, Michael John Collins senior was with the Fenians in 1867, and his grandfather was with Taigh O'Donovan in Clonakilty which was the only rising other then Emmet's rising outside Wexford in 1798. My grandmother Mary Anne O'Brien made every stitch of clothing that they all wore. She was an extraordinary woman and gave to them also the very strong character that her husband also passed on. The young Michael Collins absorbed everything the old man told him and the relationship was extraordinary because Michael Collins died when the son who was called after him was only six years old. He had already sown the seeds of love of country in him and it's a recorded fact, because I read it myself as it was written down by my aunt in 1896.

"We gathered round Dada's death bed and he said to us; 'Take care of your youngest, for one day he may do great things for Ireland".

After my grandfather Michael Collins died the young Collins transferred quite a degree of that love and affection to his eldest brother, my father Johnny, and he helped with the work on the family farm. He went to school as Lisavaird where the schoolmaster was Denis Lyons, an old Fenian. On his way home each day he passed the forge of James Santry. I mention these two men, for history will never say much about them. Denis Lyons was an extraordinary teacher and was only maintained in his position in the school because the British fortunately paid more heed to his educational abilities than to the Irish nationalism which burned within him.

Collins absorbed from Denis Lyons the love of these traditions I have mentioned earlier. Lyons saw in return, a young boy eager to learn and ask questions, and eager to use his God given intelligence. On the way home from school he would make the inevitable visit to the forge of James Santry. James had made the pikes for the 1867 rising and James's grandfather was another who was with Taigh O'Donovan in the rising at Shannonvale outside Clonakilty in 1798.

Michael Collins said one day to my father, "James Santry is one of the finest men that I have ever met".

"Why would you say that?" said my father.

"I saw", he said, "the spark from the anvil as he made the gates for all the farms around here, but I also got from him the spark he put into my heart of the love for Ireland".

It was from those two men, and from the quiet national spirit at home, that Michael Collins set out, even at that very young age, to make himself a slave to the freedom of his country.

When he dragged in a bucket of potatoes from my grandmother's garden in 1898 at the age of eight he asked my father who commended him for his extra work would he reward him by giving him truppence. My father, Johnny said

"Of course I will, but what do you want it for?".

"Dad", he said, "I've been reading lately the works of a man called Arthur Griffith which I get from James Santry".

"He is beginning to speak" he said, "at the corners of Dublin streets and telling the growing numbers of his listeners that we must not be looking to France, and Spain or the red wine of the Pope any more".

"Sinn Fein" he said, "Ourselves Alone, - that's what we must depend on".

What coincidences history throws up?. A young fellow of eight years of age who had never even been to Cork City, not to mind anywhere else, reading on the pamphlet called "Scissors and Paste" which took its name from the way the salient points that Griffith was trying to put across, were pasted on a hard board background.

34 years further on, Arthur Griffith, who was undoubtedly the most under-regarded patriot of our country, was able to say in the closing weeks of his life,

An estimated half a million people lined the funeral route to Glasnevin cemetery for the funeral of President Arthur Griffith, seen here as it passes through O'Connell Street.

"I have no ambition that my name go down in Irish History, but if it does, I want it to be associated with the name Michael Collins.

For he is the man who carried on the struggle, and after having brought it to a successful conclusion, faced the realities of the facts at that time".

Michael Collins finished his formal schooling at 12 years of age, but he was to read every play that Shakespeare wrote, the entire works of Thomas Hardey and Sir James Barrie and many other books that this great old man, his father, had collected in their home in Woodfield. Knocknagow, which he cried over, was an inspiration for him, so that he would try and ensure that its likes would not happen again in a future generation.

He had also read at the age of 12, books such as The Wealth of Nations by Adam Smith. This basic groundwork of economic thought is still valid to-day, and was in fact the text book when I did my final accountancy exam on economics. I think you will accept how unusual it was for a young fellow from Sam's Cross, Woodfield, to have read it at 12 years of age and had made notes on the side of the book of the relevant items therein to small countries such as ours.

After leaving the National School, he went on and did further studies to equip himself for the English Civil Service. That was the only job outlet in those days, for they would all have to go away in turn with the exception of Johnny, my father, his eldest brother. Michael went at the age of 16 to the Post Office in London in 1906. In his very first week over there his mother died, but sadly he had no money with which to return home for his mother's funeral. He, along with his sister Hannie and their second cousin Nancy O'Brien went to Mass for their mother at Brompton Oratory. This was the very same church to which he went to attend daily Mass during those Treaty negotiation days fifteen years later.

Collins went to many plays in London and widened the scope of his reading.

He attended three hour classes to improve his reading of English on three nights a week, and also took classes about conferring one's thoughts to paper in a concise fashion. He wrote essay after essay, - two of which are reprinted on the following page, while below is a reprint from one of his copybooks showing his clear handwriting style.

Collins threw himself into the Gaelic League in London. He joined the Geraldines Hurling and Football Club and soon became its Secretary. He was enrolled into the IRB by the man whose name is now famous on the All- Ireland Football Trophy, - Sam Maguire. But I believe one of the greatest benefits he had in London at that time was his sister Hannie who lived in Kensington Gardens. She had preceded him by several years and was now gaining promotion in the British Civil Service. She took the words of her father to heart and right to her dying day, she too was a voracious reader.

Done under exam rules;
Time 1½ hours

M J Collins
I

'Nothing Venture nothing Have'

Amidst all the wealth of proverbial lore there is probably no healthier maxim to impress upon the young than 'Nothing Venture nothing Have'. It gives emphasis to the fact that no great and noteworthy achievement was ever attained without exertion and ambition.

Extracts from two essays written by General Michael Collins while a young student in London.

CONTENTMENT IS BETTER THAN RICHES.

"A content mind" it has been said "is a continual feast". It would indeed be difficult to overestimate the value of this rare quality, for after all, a man's happiness depends less upon his good or bad fortune than upon the way in which he bears it. Many a poor, sick child subject to a life-long legacy of suffering, is brighter and happier than some pampered heir of fortune whose every whim is humoured at whatever cost.

Money has been called the root of all evil. Of course this is only so when the power money brings is abused, but when rightly used it may be a great power for good. Generally speaking riches are often found to be a clog on virtue. Hence Christ's saying that it is easier for a camel to pass through the eye of a needle than for a rich man to enter into the kingdom of God.

Bacon compared riches to the baggage of an army. He said as baggage hindereth the march, and even sometimes the care of it loseth or disturbth the victory, so were riches to virtue. He also added that there were no real uses for great riches except in distribution. Moreover the rich man is invariably anxious for the safety of his treasures.

Happiness consists of the fewness of our wants. We want but little here below, nor want that little long. If abundance comes let us be thankful for it, but if that is not our lot we should avoid the wishing for it or indeed anything we do not possess.

"NOTHING VENTURE NOTHING HAVE"

Amidst all the wealth of proverbial lore there is probably no healthier maxim to impress upon the young than "Nothing Venture Nothing Have" It gives emphasis to the fact that no great or noteworthy achievement was ever attained without exertion and ambition. At first sight this doctrine seems a rather bitter pill to swallow. However a slight consideration of the apophthegm will convince us of its truth. We have only to look around us and see how many of the failures in life are due to the fault of blindly and fatuously trusting in "luck". To wait passively for good fortune to smile on us, is like waiting for a stream to run dry. It is true that good luck knocks at least once at each man's door, but the tide must be taken at the flood, and in a lively and vigorous manner.

In the history of the world's famous men we find that all of them were ready to venture even their existence on the attainment of their ends. Washington played a large stake, and it was only by venturing everything that he was master of, that he won it. The same was true of Garibaldi in Italy, and in England, Richard 3rd. unfeelingly sacrificed his nephews because they were in his way to the throne.

We must not however be too rash. It has been tactfully said that "vaulting ambition o'erleaps itself" and history is rich in instances of this truth.

Napoleon aspired to being emporor of Europe, but Waterloo made him a prisoner and an exile, and so forever barred him from being anything greater that an inhabitant of a cell in St. Helena.

Fire, when kept under restraint, is a useful servant, but when it gets the upper mand it is a merciless tyrant. The same holds good of ambition. If we take it to mean an unquenchable desire to advance by honest methods towards perfection, it is one of the best qualities a man can be endowed with.

Michael's brother Johnnie married the legendary Nancy O'Brien following the death of his first wife. This is their son Michael's (front right) account of a dramatic period of Ireland's history.

His second cousin Nancy O'Brien, who also worked in the post office, was astonished at the improvement in expressing himself and in putting his thoughts together in writing. He would give her essays to constructively criticise and she, who was the same age as himself would ask, "What is this all about Michael ? ".

"Nancy" he said, "If I am to ever lead my country to freedom I will want to know how to express myself, how to put words on the overriding conviction I have, that instead of being a victim of happenings, I will cause things to happen. I will then practice for as long as it takes me to express myself clearly without notes, because in speaking from a written script, the heart isn't in the words. The nuances of the word, and the inspiration in the words come from the heart and they have to be expressed through that most errant organ, the tongue". These are extraordinary expressions for a man of 17 and 18, and that is what he gave himself unswervingly to do.

Often he would have liked to gone out with the lads, or to have gone with Nancy O'Brien and his sister Hannie to the plays, but Collins was keeping an eye on developments back home in Ireland. He was securing and bringing his potential slowly to its fuller development.

When word of the rising came he returned to Dublin and was Aide de Camp to James Plunkett in the GPO in 1916. I don't know, how many people have read his comments on it, - "It was the greatest bloody fiasco that we ever were engaged in. There was courage, there was patriotism but there was bloody all else. There was no organisation".

continued on page 61

Lower O'Connell Street as it looked before 1916.

AN ILLUSTRATED RECORD

OF THE

SINN FEIN REVOLT IN DUBLIN

APRIL 1916

Photograph by Mr. Geo. D. Gray, B.A.I.,
Assistant Engineer, Dublin Corporation.

SACKVILLE STREET AND EDEN QUAY AFTER THE REVOLT

Published by permission of Mr M. J. Buckley,
Borough Surveyor.

RUINS IN SACKVILLE ST. DUBLIN

CHANCELLOR, DUBLIN.

LOWER SACKVILLE ST. DUBLIN.

G.P.O. SACKVILLE ST., DUBLIN.

CHANCELLOR, DUBLIN.

CHANCELLOR DUBLIN   LIBERTY HALL. HEAD-QUARTERS OF CITIZEN ARMY, DUBLIN.

DIARY OF PRINCIPAL EVENTS.

EASTER MONDAY, APRIL 24th.

At twelve o'clock noon, General Post Office seized by Insurgents.

Corner houses at North Earl Street, Henry Street, Abbey Street, Middle and Lower, seized and barricaded.

Publication of Proclamation of Irish Republic and flag hoisted on G.P.O.

St. Stephen's Green seized; gates closed and barricaded.

College of Surgeons seized and a garrison placed therein.

Attack made at Dublin Castle on the guard house at Upper Castle Gate.

The City Hall, *Daily Express* Office and opposite corner house at Parliament Street raided and occupied by armed forces.

The Four Courts seized by strong party; entrances and windows barricaded

South Dublin Union and Roe's Distillery Stores occupied.

Boland's Mills at Ringsend and the Distillery at the same place seized. Pickets placed on railway line near Lansdowne Road.

W. & R. Jacob's Biscuit Factory raided and occupied.

Attack on body of Lancers in Sackville Street; three shot.

Attack from houses at Northumberland Road on G.R. Veterans' Corps returning from route march; five killed.

Numerous street barricades erected.

Westland Row Station seized and occupied.

Harcourt Street Station seized, but later in evening abandoned.

Broadstone Station seized; military officers travelling arrested.

Kingsbridge Station raided; military eject insurgents and hold station.

Unsuccessful attempt to seize Amiens Street Station.

Looting begins in Sackville Street; sweet shops and boot shops first to suffer.

Fighting in progress in Dolphin's Barn and other outlying places.

Fighting at Portobello Bridge; numerous casualties.

Magazine Fort raided by armed party and set on fire.

TUESDAY, 25th APRIL.

Abortive attempts made in early morning to blow up Nelson's Pillar.

Looting increases, mainly in Sackville Street.

Lawrence's toy shop sacked and set on fire.

Bridges and points of entry to city barricaded.

Military attacks at barricades near Cabra and Charleville Road; forty casualties reported; 100 prisoners taken by military.

Unsuccessful attempt to blow up Cabra Bridge and bridge crossing railway on North Circular Road.

Attempt to blow up Great Northern Railway at Fairview.

Heavy fighting at Cork Hill between rebels and military at Parliament Street and at the Castle.

Insurgents driven from *Daily Express* Offices, Cork Hill, by military at point of the bayonet.

Authorities proclaim Martial Law.

Military reinforcements arrive; general plans formulated, and attack on G.P.O. begun.

General Sir John Maxwell appointed Commander of Forces.

Aerial erected over the Wireless School at Reis' building in Sackville Street, occupied by the Insurgents.

Issue of the Insurgent paper, the "Irish War News."

WEDNESDAY, 26th APRIL.

Large reinforcements of infantry and artillery arrive from England.

Bombardment of Liberty Hall and Boland's Mills by the *Helga*.

Liberty Hall rushed and occupied by the military.

Heavy fighting in Sackville Street; military attack G.P.O.

Kelly's shop, corner of Bachelor's Walk, attacked by artillery and machine guns.

Attack on the Sherwood Foresters arriving from Kingstown, at Mount Street Bridge.

Martial Law proclaimed to extend to whole of Ireland.

THURSDAY, 27th APRIL.

Further arrival of troops from England.

Insurgents bombed out of stronghold in Clanwilliam Place.

Fire breaks out in the forenoon at Wynn's Hotel in Lower Abbey Street.

FRIDAY, 28th APRIL.

The attack on the G.P.O. develops, artillery brought to bear; fire breaks out in the building and burns throughout the night.

SATURDAY, 29th APRIL.

Fire breaks out on the western side of Sackville Street.

At four o'clock the military order "Cease Firing."

General surrender of Sinn Fein forces in city and county ordered by P. H. Pearse and submitted to military.

Surrender, unconditionally, of James Connolly and forces under his command.

Surrender at Four Courts.

Departure of first batch of 489 prisoners to England.

SUNDAY, 30th APRIL.

Surrender at College of Surgeons by Countess Markievicz.

Surrender at Jacob's and South Dublin Union.

Surrender at one o'clock at Boland's Mills.

Desultory sniping took place at Sandymount, Ringsend and other outlying districts during the ensuing week.

THE SINN FEIN REVOLT, APRIL, 1916

On Easter Monday, April 24th, at mid-day, when a compact body of men, mostly in uniform and carrying arms, swung out of Abbey Street into Sackville Street, little notice was taken by the few people in the neighbourhood. It was indeed a familiar sight in Dublin, particularly so on a holiday, and occasioned little comment and no apprehension. The curiosity of those who had noticed in their morning paper a paragraph intimating that Mr. Eoin McNeill, the President of the Irish Volunteers, had cancelled the Easter manœuvres and forbidden any parades, found explanation in the fact that the body of men referred to came from the direction of Beresford Place, and were probably therefore "Citizen Army" men, who were regarded by most people as being independent of the Volunteer commands.

A prompt "halt" and "left turn" bringing the men opposite to and facing the G.P.O., attracted attention, which gave place to consternation when the ranks were broken, and at the "double" a rush was made for the new entrance of the public office. Those members of the public who were within transacting business were naturally greatly alarmed at what had taken place, and it appears to have taken some revolver shooting to bring realisation to them that serious disturbances were afoot. The building was quickly emptied of public and officials, and an armed guard placed at the entrance. All glass in the windows on the three sides facing the streets was broken, and barricades were quickly improvised with furniture, mail bags and articles of all kinds from the offices. Presently a man in uniform emerges and pastes up on the door a copy of the Proclamation of the

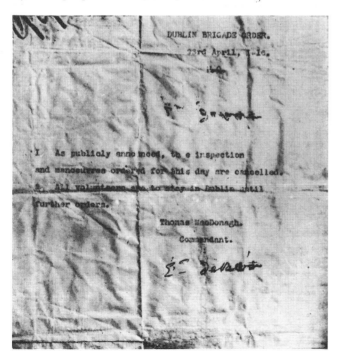

Headquarters Order cancelling the Easter Manœuvres of the Irish Volunteers.

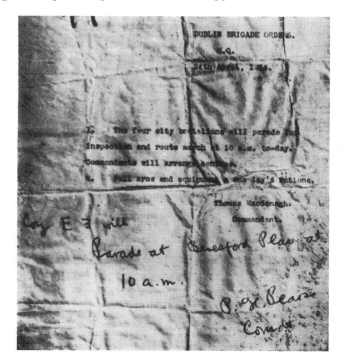

Subsequent Order for a Parade and Route March on Easter Monday with full arms.—Countersigned by P. H. Pearse.

Irish Republic, and to the accompaniment of volleys of shots, the colours of the Republic of Ireland were broken on the flagstaff at the northern corner of the building. By 12.20 the telegraph cables were severed, and so far as the G.P.O. was concerned, Dublin was isolated from the external world.

Shortly after the occupation the first encounter with military occurred. A troop of Lancers who were, it appears, escorting four or five waggons of ammunition, crossed from the Eden Quay side of Sackville Street up Bachelor's Walk. Having deposited their charge in a position of comparative safety they returned to Sackville Street, entering from the northern end. As soon as they reached the G.P.O. they were met with a volley from the roof of the building, and four of the party were shot; two of their horses lay in the street for some days, forming a gruesome and warlike reminder of the incident.

Meanwhile, steps were taken to seize and garrison various houses at the corners of the streets abutting Sackville Street, as supporting defences. In this way the overhead premises of the Hibernian Bank and the opposite corner of Lower Abbey Street, over which was situated the Wireless Telegraphy School, were early in the hands of the insurgents. Across the street Messrs. Manfield's fine premises and the opposite corner of Middle Abbey Street were similarly placed in a position of defence. The windows in all these

POBLACHT NA H EIREANN.

THE PROVISIONAL GOVERNMENT
OF THE
IRISH REPUBLIC
TO THE PEOPLE OF IRELAND.

IRISHMEN AND IRISHWOMEN : In the name of God and of the dead generations from which she receives her old tradition of nationhood, Ireland, through us, summons her children to her flag and strikes for her freedom.

Having organised and trained her manhood through her secret revolutionary organisation, the Irish Republican Brotherhood, and through her open military organisations, the Irish Volunteers and the Irish Citizen Army, having patiently perfected her discipline, having resolutely waited for the right moment to reveal itself, she now seizes that moment, and, supported by her exiled children in America and by gallant allies in Europe, but relying in the first on her own strength, she strikes in full confidence of victory.

We declare the right of the people of Ireland to the ownership of Ireland, and to the unfettered control of Irish destinies, to be sovereign and indefeasible. The long usurpation of that right by a foreign people and government has not extinguished the right, nor can it ever be extinguished except by the destruction of the Irish people. In every generation the Irish people have asserted their right to national freedom and sovereignty; six times during the past three hundred years they have asserted it in arms. Standing on that fundamental right and again asserting it in arms in the face of the world, we hereby proclaim the Irish Republic as a Sovereign Independent State, and we pledge our lives and the lives of our comrades-in-arms to the cause of its freedom, of its welfare, and of its exaltation among the nations.

The Irish Republic is entitled to, and hereby claims, the allegiance of every Irishman and Irishwoman. The Republic guarantees religious and civil liberty, equal rights and equal opportunities to all its citizens, and declares its resolve to pursue the happiness and prosperity of the whole nation and of all its parts, cherishing all the children of the nation equally, and oblivious of the differences carefully fostered by an alien government, which have divided a minority from the majority in the past.

Until our arms have brought the opportune moment for the establishment of a permanent National Government, representative of the whole people of Ireland and elected by the suffrages of all her men and women, the Provisional Government, hereby constituted, will administer the civil and military affairs of the Republic in trust for the people.

We place the cause of the Irish Republic under the protection of the Most High God, Whose blessing we invoke upon our arms, and we pray that no one who serves that cause will dishonour it by cowardice, inhumanity, or rapine. In this supreme hour the Irish nation must, by its valour and discipline and by the readiness of its children to sacrifice themselves for the common good, prove itself worthy of the august destiny to which it is called.

Signed on Behalf of the Provisional Government,

THOMAS J. CLARKE.
SEAN Mac DIARMADA.   THOMAS MacDONAGH.
P. H. PEARSE.   EAMONN CEANNT.
JAMES CONNOLLY.   JOSEPH PLUNKETT.

The Proclamation of the Provisional Government issued at the G.P.O. on Monday, 24th April.

premises were broken and barricaded with every kind of furniture and fittings that the house or offices would afford. The tram service was stopped; one car being derailed at the entrance of North Earl Street formed the nucleus of a street barricade. It was presently supplemented by furniture, shop fittings and goods of all kinds taken from the neighbouring houses. Barricades were erected in all the adjoining streets; one at the Sackville Street end of Lower Abbey Street consisted mainly of bicycles and tyres from Kelly's and Keating's premises close by, supplemented by many rolls of " news " taken from the *Irish Times'* paper stores. At the Hibernian Bank corner of Lower Abbey Street elaborate preparations were made. This was subsequently found to be due to the special precautions necessary for the defence of the opposite corner, which is the Wireless School referred to in Mr. James Connolly's Order (which we reproduce) as " our Wireless Station." The aerial here was dismantled by the military on the outbreak of the European War. It was replaced in position on the outbreak of the revolt, and it is said that wireless messages were being constantly despatched until the destruction of the building by fire on Thursday night. The corners of Sackville Street at Bachelor's Walk and Eden Quay were occupied in great strength, being important positions commanding the approaches to the central position from the south side of the

John McDermott.

Thomas J. Clarke.

Patrick H. Pearse.

Eamonn Ceannt.

Six of the Signatories to the Proclamation of the Provisional Government:

JOHN McDERMOTT was a native of Leitrim, and was one of the founders of the Volunteer movement. He was associated with some of the advanced papers that had sprung up in Dublin in furtherance of the ideas of the extreme section among the Volunteers, and was editor of *Irish Freedom*. He was tried by court-martial and executed on May 12th.

THOMAS J. CLARKE represented the old Fenian conspiracy on the Provisional Government. He had been convicted of association with the dynamite outrages in England in the eighties, and sentenced to penal servitude. On his release he returned to Dublin, and opened a small tobacco and newspaper shop near the Rotunda. He was sentenced by court-martial to death, and executed on May 3rd.

PATRICK H. PEARSE was born thirty-six years ago in Dublin, of English parentage. He was a member of the Irish Bar, and was Principal of St. Enda's School for boys at Rathfarnham, Co. Dublin. He was Commandant-General of the Army of the Irish Republic and President of the Provisional Government. Tried by court-martial, he was sentenced to death, and executed on May 3rd.

EAMONN CEANNT held a responsible position in the Treasury Department of Dublin Corporation. He was a man of considerable mental attainments, and was a prominent member of the Gaelic League. Following the sentence of court-martial he was executed on May 8th.

THOMAS MACDONAGH was a native of Cloughjordan. He was an M.A. of the National University of Ireland and a tutor of English literature in the University College, Dublin. He was associated with P. H. Pearse in conducting St. Enda's School. Tried by court-martial and sentenced to death, he was executed on May 3rd.

JOSEPH PLUNKETT, twenty-eight years of age, was at one time the editor of a monthly publication which has now ceased, called the *Irish Review*. He had written a good deal of distinguished work both in prose and verse. A pathetic circumstance in his case was his marriage in prison on the eve of his execution. Tried by court-martial he was sentenced to death, and executed on May 4th.

[JAMES CONNOLLY's portrait appears in the section dealing with Liberty Hall.]

Thomas MacDonagh.

Joseph Plunkett.

Photos by Lafayette and Keogh Bros.

ARMY OF THE IRISH REPUBLIC

(Dublin Command)

Headquarters

Date..25th April,. 1916

To

Officer in Charge, Reis & D.B.C

The main purpose of your post is to protect our wireless station. Its secondary purpose is to observe
Lower Abbey Street and Lower O'Connell Street. Commandeer
in the D.B.C. whatever food and utensils you require.
Make sure of a plentiful supply of water wherever your
men are. Break all glass in the windows of the rooms

occupied by you for fighting purpose. Establish a
connection between your forces in the D.B.C. and in
Reis' building. Be sure that the stairways leading
immediately to your rooms are well barracaded. We have
a post in the house at the corner Bachelor's Walk, in
the Hotel Metropole, in the Imperial Hotel, in General
Post Office. The directions from which you are likely
to be attacked are from the Custom House or from the
far side of the river, Dolier Street or Westmoreland Street
We believe there is a sniper in McBurneys on the far
side of the river

James Connolly

Commandant General

Order of James Connolly, Commandant-General Insurgent Forces, issued from Headquarters at G.P.O.

river. This was the position on Monday evening so far as the Sackville Street area was concerned. Meanwhile firing was heard from other parts of the city, mainly from the direction of Dublin Castle.

At this point the initial steps were much the same as at the G.P.O. A small body of insurgents, numbering not more than fourteen, marched up Dame Street to Cork Hill, and turning to the left approached the Upper Castle Gate. Here was but one policeman and a sentry. The sentry apparently thinking the small body of Volunteers intended passing quietly up Castle Street, took no notice until the turn was made as if to enter the Castle Gate. The constable, James O'Brien, 168 B, then advanced with upraised hand : he was immediately shot dead. Other shots were fired at the sentry inside the railings and at the guardroom. The iron gates were quickly closed, whereupon a bomb, consisting of a loaded tin canister, was flung over the railings at the guardroom window which it broke, but failing to explode did no further harm. The insurgents, foiled here, broke up, some making for the City Hall, climbing the railings and gaining entry ; others passing into the *Daily Express* offices, and the remainder into Henry & James' premises at the opposite corner. The original small party must have received considerable reinforcements, as when the *Express* offices were eventually taken by the military on Wednesday, 26 dead bodies were found on the premises.

The fighting in Parliament St. developed into a guerilla campaign carried from house to house. Tunnelling, by blasting passages through internal walls, was freely adopted by the insurgents. The fronts of many of the premises on the eastern side of the street, notably the Royal Exchange Hotel, indicate the intensity of the attack.

Headquarters instructions for equipment of Officers and Men
Irish Volunteers.

The Upper Gate, Dublin Castle, showing the Guardroom on right.

Sean Connolly.
Shot leading the attack on Dublin Castle.

After the entry of the insurgents to the City Hall, a number were seen
on the roof. With full advantage of the parapet, snipers took up positions
commanding the likely approaches of the military. Parliament Street as
far as Grattan Bridge was bullet-swept on the sight of a khaki uniform.
A figure on the roof was presently seen from below to struggle with the
staff that usually carries the municipal flag, and in a few moments the
Republican colours were hoisted. This was scarcely done when a fusilade
of shots rang out, and the figure was seen to double up. The building was
soon stormed by the military, and the insurgent colours torn down. This
is said to have been the flag intended to hang over Dublin Castle, and was
borne by Sean Connolly, who led the attack which was destined to proceed
no further than the outer gate.

Some organising ability marked the seizure of Stephen's Green, whatever may be said of the judgment exercised in its selection as a position with any hope of being held. The insurgents reached its gates in twos and threes, and at a signal entered and closed them, being equipped with chains and locks for securing them. Small parties scattered through the Park gathering members of the public and driving them out, while others were quickly preparing shallow rifle pits in the soft banked earth of the shrubberies round the railings. Officers meanwhile sought out points of vantage in the surrounding houses for the placing of snipers for the defence of the position, and these were quickly assigned their posts. A large body, said to be under the command of the Countess Markievicz, entered the College of Surgeons, and this building appears to have been selected as the main guard.

On Tuesday the military took up positions in the Shelbourne Hotel and other houses overlooking the Park, and a vigorous sniping of the rebels followed. Ultimately the position of those occupying the trenches round the railings became untenable, and a withdrawal towards more central and less exposed points of defence became necessary. It was not, however, till towards the end of the week that the Park was evacuated, and then numbers of the rebel forces were enabled to make good their escape either into the College of Surgeons or other contiguous houses, from which persistent sniping continued.

A member of the Inner Temple, who was besieged in the Shelbourne Hotel, relates that some of the guests were taken prisoners by the insurgents, but most of them were released after a few hours and allowed to return to the Hotel. A luggage porter who was too slow for them was shot. " At five o'clock on Tuesday morning," he proceeds, " I was awakened and told that the military were in occupation

Little's Publichouse, at foot of Harcourt Street. One of the important points of Defence for Stephen's Green.

St. Stephen's Green (from Shelbourne Hotel) Dublin.

of the Hotel and were firing on the rebels in the Green. I quickly dressed, and made my way along the corridors crowded with guests in all stages of attire. Continuous firing was going on from the windows of the Hotel, and replies came from the Green. A body of eighty soldiers with a machine gun had made their way from the Castle between 1 a.m. and 3 a.m., had taken up their position at the windows, and opened fire at dawn. The front entrance had been barricaded with mattresses, tables and chairs, and at nearly every window a soldier was stationed with a rifle. By 8 o'clock firing gradually ceased, and the Green appeared to be empty ; the dead were picked up. Comparatively little happened during the day, except that a machine gun kept a constant

Photo by T. W. Murphy.

fire on the College of Surgeons to the right. When we retired to bed that night a large portion of the guests slept in the corridors in their ordinary clothes. The following day a sortie was made, and captures were made of about 60 service rifles, a dozen shot guns of all kinds, between a dozen and twenty bombs, two motor bicycles and six ordinary bicycles."

It was at the beginning of operations that Constable M. Lahiff was killed. He was on duty at the Grafton Street entrance to the Park, and was ordered away by the insurgents. Refusing to desert his post, one of the rebels raising his rifle shot him dead.

Mr. W. H. Ashmore, M.P.S.I., relates an exciting experience during the period of the occupation of Stephen's Green by the insurgents. With three others he was made prisoner, and confined in the greenhouse in the grounds of the Park. Here he was compelled to render first aid to the " garrison," being a certified member of the British Red Cross Society— a fact disclosed by his button-badge. Mr. Ashmore makes no complaint of his treatment at the hands of the rebels.

After a week's occupation the surrender of the College of Surgeons took place at two o'clock in the afternoon of Sunday, the 30th April. Major Wheeler, son of the late Surgeon Wheeler, accompanied by a force of military, attended at that hour, and was received by the rebel leader,

Countess Markievicz found scope for her enthusiasm in a variety of causes. She was at one time prominent in the suffragette movement. Latterly she was closely identified with labour troubles in Dublin, being a trusted colleague of James Larkin. She was in command, in male attire, at the College of Surgeons during the revolt, and surrendered with over a hundred of her detachment on Sunday, April 30th. Her trial by Court-martial took place on 5th May, when she was sentenced to death, this being later commuted to penal servitude for life.

See page 103

COLLEGE OF SURGEONS, ST. STEPHEN'S GREEN, DUBLIN.

Sean Connolly and the Countess Markievicz, as they appeared in a Play " The Memory of the Dead," written by Count Markievicz. Connolly, who took part in the revolt, was killed in the attack on the Castle.

the Countess Markievicz. She was still wearing top boots, breeches, service tunic and a hat with feathers. In the presence of the military she first shook hands with her " officers," and then produced her revolver, which was enclosed in a case. After affectionately kissing the weapon she handed it to Major Wheeler, together with a quantity of ammunition.

The prisoners taken at this place numbered about one hundred and ten men and young women.

Edward Daly, Commandant of the Volunteers, in charge
of the operations at the Four Courts.
Executed by sentence of Court-martial, May 4th, 1916.

The Four Courts.

Photos by Keogh Bros. and T. W. Murphy.

The Four Courts was regarded by the insurgent forces as a point of great importance, and was, like the G.P.O., placed in a condition strong alike for offence and defence. Investigation of the premises after evacuation led to the conclusion that a large force must have been in possession. The gates were closed and barricaded on Monday with all manner of furniture and articles from the Courts and offices. The windows were defended by ramparts of volumes from the Law Library. The supporting points for the Four Courts were the Mendicity Institute on the west, and the houses at the corner of Bridge Street on the east, at the south side of the river. The former was taken by the military on the Monday, the latter burnt down. The passage of the quays, particularly on the northern side, was extremely dangerous. Church Street Bridge was barricaded, and sentries posted there. The fighting in this quarter was of a desultory, sniping character. The resistance at the Four Courts came to an end on Saturday, when the insurgents surrendered. Edward Daly was in command here.

It will be learned with relief that the building and the valuable records are nearly intact. A great deal of glass has, of course, been broken, and the furniture, books, and documents in many of the departments have been used to form barricades for the snipers. Attempts appear to have been made by the rebels to investigate the contents of the safes in the offices, but their efforts proved unsuccessful, except in the case of the safe in the Law Library which, however, was empty.

A large number of workmen were engaged restoring the place to its normal state, but this will necessarily occupy some time. In the course of this work four unexploded bombs were discovered in the Library. They were at once removed to a place of safety.

Corner of Four Courts at Chancery Place, showing injury by
shell and rifle fire.

This high building overlooking the Grand Canal Basin and the drawbridge formed at once a commanding position eminently lending itself to attack or defence, and well secured against any scarcity of provender. Events justified its selection by the insurgents, as it proved one of the most difficult positions to overcome. Seized on the Monday, it was quickly and easily barricaded by plentiful sacks of flour—an admirable bulwark against bullets. A flank defence was provided by the old Distillery on the other side of the drawbridge. Pickets were also placed in a field near the Gas Works and on the railway line between Lansdowne Road and Westland Row Station. The position was eminently suited also for attack upon Beggar's Bush Barracks, which lies within easy reach, and here, during the week, unfortunate casualties took place. No provision could be made against the attack of the nine-pounder on the gunboat *Helga*, which was used against the mill from the Liffey at Ringsend on Wednesday.

On Thursday an artillery duel took place between a couple of naval guns placed near the Grand Canal and the rebels stationed in the City Distillery on Ringsend Road, in which they had two guns of heavy calibre. Firing opened at 5 o'clock, and for twenty minutes the battle raged, the rebels replying vigorously to the attack until the military found the range, when a well-directed shell knocked out one of the guns and the green flag which up to then had floated over the building. The next shot from the naval gun dismantled the second gun of the rebels, and the

Edward de Valera. Born in New York of Spanish descent. Educated in Blackrock College, he was a Bachelor of Arts, and a Professor of Mathematics. He was Commandant in charge of the operations in the Ringsend district, and surrendered with 100 men on Sunday, April 30. Sentence of death passed upon him on May 11th, was commuted to penal servitude for life.

duel was over. Part of Boland's " fort " was the clinker heaps in the gas tank fields, and in them the rebels were entrenched all the week. The snipers here gave the military a lot of trouble, and the toll of casualties was very heavy.

On Friday and Saturday the spirits of the rebels in the mill are said to have been much depressed, and many of them expressed a desire to get home.

The final surrender of the garrison of 100 men at Boland's was made by de Valera, who was Rebel Commandant, on Sunday at one o'clock, but detached parties of snipers in the locality continued fighting, mainly from the railway, until the following Monday. Afterwards those who remained at large worked their way round into the Sandymount district, where desultory firing was maintained at intervals for days afterwards.

It is said that the bakers at Boland's were made prisoners and compelled to bake bread for the insurgents during the occupation.

The rebels in the mill numbered eighty. During the week twelve of them were wounded and six killed.

Boland's Mills at Ringsend, a stronghold of the Insurgents. Surrendered on Sunday, April 30th

Photos by T. W. Murphy and Keogh Bros

From a strategical point of view the selection of W. & R. Jacob's fine factory in Bishop Street would not seem to recommend itself to soldiers of experience, except as a food depot. Even in this respect the readiness with which its approach could be controlled would limit its utility except for those within its walls. Its attraction from the insurgents' point of view lay possibly in the facilities it afforded for attack upon Ship Street Barracks, which lies between it and the Castle, and upon which heavy fire was maintained. The congested neighbourhood surrounding the factory hampered the attack of the military, and when the wearing out tactics they adopted began to take effect, the same conditions favoured the escape of many who would otherwise have been made prisoners. The surrender was made upon Sunday night, 30th April, having been brought

Major John McBride organised the Irish Brigade on the side of the Boers in the South African War, was a native of Westport, Co. Mayo. He threw over the Irish constitutional party in 1895, and joined the physical force party. He was a man of good education, and was intended for the medical profession. In 1911 he was appointed by the Dublin Corporation to the position of water bailiff. Major McBride was in command of the insurgents at Jacob's Factory, and surrendered on Sunday night, the 30th April. He was tried by Court-martial, sentenced to death, and executed on May 6th.

Front of W. & R. Jacob's premises in Peter's Row.

Photos by T. W. Murphy and Keogh Bros.

about by a member of the Carmelite Order from Whitefriar Street as intermediary. Amid the cheers of the crowd gathered about the building, the clergyman was hoisted by a number of men up to one of the lower windows, from which the bags of flour used instead of sand by the rebels had been pulled. He went inside the factory, and not long after a party of Volunteers walked out. The garrison, leaving their flag flying, came out of the factory one by one on Sunday night, many of them dressed in civilian attire which had been passed in to them by their friends at the rear of the factory.

It is pleasant to record that in this instance where great injury to the valuable machinery in the biscuit factory might have been caused, if wilful damage had been desired, practically no harm was done.

After the surrender some looting took place, bags of flour and boxes of biscuits being carried off.

The South Dublin Union, where Commandant Eamon Ceannt was in charge of the rebel forces, appears to have been seized to form a centre for the operations in a large area, including Dolphin's Barn, Marrowbone Lane, Watling Street, Kilmainham, Rialto and Inchicore. Messrs. Roe's Malting Stores at Mount Brown were early occupied, but the insurgents were driven out on Wednesday, making their way along the small river that flows through the district, in an attempt to reach the open country. The majority of these, however, were rounded up and lodged in Kilmainham Prison. Obvious difficulty was experienced by the military in dealing with the insurgents, who stubbornly held out in the offices of the Union. The presence of many helpless inmates in the institution prevented the adoption of methods of attack that would otherwise have brought the conflict here to a speedy termination. A surrender was not reached until Sunday night, April 30th. Large batches of prisoners arriving at Kilmainham Jail were greeted by the crowd with marked hostility.

The attack upon the Magazine in the Phœnix Park may be regarded as coming within the operations of this sphere of conflict. An armed party, driving up to the Fort through the Island Bridge Gate, overpowered the sentry, and covering with a revolver Mrs. Playfair, the wife of the Commandant, who resided in the building, demanded the whereabouts of the telephone, which was promptly dismantled. Six minutes was given to the inmates in which to clear out before the place was blown up. The elder of Mrs. Playfair's boys rushed out, making his way to Park Place, from whence he could telephone for assistance. The lad's mission was detected, and just as he had arrived at his destination he was shot dead by one of the raiding party, who had followed him on a bicycle. By this time the rebels at the Fort, with the intention of carrying out their threat to explode the contents of the Magazine, had set fire to the outer portion of it, and having done so, apparently fearing their own destruction from the result, hurried away. Military assistance now arrived, and immediate attempts were made to combat the fire. The Brigade being summoned, it was got under, fortunately before reaching the compartment in which the high explosives were kept, the section destroyed being a store containing small arms only.

The insurgents' tenure of Broadstone Station was a short if somewhat

PHŒNIX PARK, DUBLIN. (ISLAND·BRIDGE·ENTRANCE.)

The entrance to the Phœnix Park used by the party that raided the Magazine Fort.

exciting one. After seizure on Monday, a number of military officers returning from Fairyhouse Races were a windfall to the insurgents in occupation. They were promptly made prisoners and detained in the station until next day, when the premises were retaken by the military.

The original party seizing Westland Row Station did not comprise more than thirty in number. Taking the public and the staff of the station completely by surprise, by ten minutes past twelve on Monday the station was in their hands. The last train was the twelve o'clock local, after which there was no train in or out of Westland Row during the day. The telephone and telegraphic instruments throughout the station were cut off, and barricades speedily erected at the goods and passenger entrances and the carriageway.

Harcourt Street was taken at 12.5 p.m., and the premises barricaded, but at about 3 p.m. the Volunteers abandoned the position, and the railway officials resumed duties. Outside the station obstructions had been laid upon the line, but these were easily removed, and a train left at 5.30 and another at 6.15.

PORTOBELLO BRIDGE AND HOSPITAL, DUBLIN.

severe test could be offered to seasoned soldiers than to find themselves ambushed in a strange locality affording little or no cover and swept by a veritable hail of bullets from all directions. Skilfully selected houses commanding all the likely approaches had been seized and garrisoned, and so well was the ambush managed that the unsuspecting advanced guard was permitted to proceed in safety past the points of attack. When the main body came within range volley after volley was fired into the ranks from Clanwilliam Place. With a promptitude and resource worthy of old campaigners these young troops quickly realised the situation, and a hot reply was made to the insurgents' fire.

It was, however, on Easter Monday that fighting was begun in this neighbourhood. Several companies of the Veterans' Volunteer Corps returning from Ticknock, where they had been route marching, had scarcely turned out of Northumberland Road into Haddington Road on their way to Headquarters at Beggar's Bush Barracks, when the first companies were met with a fusilade from snipers established in adjoining houses. The Corps, in uniform and carrying rifles, was without ammunition, and was therefore at the mercy of the attacking party. A portion attempted to regain the barracks by Lansdowne Road, but these, too, were sniped at by a party of insurgents occupying the railway bridge over

The bridge at Portobello was seized by a rebel force after mid-day on Monday, Davy's publichouse being selected as the most suitable fort for its defence. A garrison was quickly installed and the windows barricaded. An unsuspecting military officer, returning to the neighbouring barracks from the city, was immediately fired upon, but fortunately escaping unhurt he reached the barracks and ordered out a strong armed guard. This at once drew the fire of the insurgents, which was returned, the soldiers availing of such scanty cover as the place afforded. Strong reinforcements with machine guns quickly arriving, an attack upon the publichouse was decided upon. Led by a senior officer the military soon gained access to the building by employing the butt-ends of their rifles to the doors. A search of the premises was disappointing to the soldiers ; the facilities to escape in many directions had been fully availed of. The military remained in charge of the building and neighbourhood. The illustration shows Portobello Hospital to the left and Davy's publichouse in the centre of the picture.

On Wednesday fighting of a most vicious and sanguinary character took place in the Mount Street neighbourhood on the arrival of the first of the reinforcements of British troops from Kingstown. It fell to the lot of the Sherwood Foresters to here undergo their first ordeal. The battalion was made up of young troops for the first time under fire, and no more

G. R. Veterans' Corps at the review at Trinity College
Inspected by Gen. Sir John Maxwell.

The scene of the battle at Clanwilliam Place, Mount Street Bridge, where the Sherwood Foresters suffered so severely.

The defence of Trinity College will certainly remain one of the most creditable traditions of the Institution. This position, commanding the heart of the city, of the utmost strategical importance, in the hands of the insurgents might have become to them one of enormous advantage. When the Insurrection broke out the number of the Dublin University Officers' Training Corps in College was actually eight all told. With most praiseworthy energy this small garrison proceeded to put the place in a state of defence. The gates were shut, arms served out, the windows facing College Green sandbagged, and the few defenders so placed in them as to give the utmost appearance of strength and numbers. Steps were immediately taken to summon those of the Corps within reach, and so ready and quick was the response that by seven o'clock on Monday the army of defence reached a total of forty-four men. When it is realised that a successful defending of the College against entry meant the guarding of fronts at Nassau Street, Brunswick Street, College Street and Bath Avenue. The casualties included the following members of the Corps :—Killed : F. H. Browning, Thomas Harborne, Reginald Clery, James Nolan, John Gibbs. G. Hosford, another of the Corps, was shot while in Beggar's Bush Barracks by a sniper on Wednesday, 26th April. Members of the Corps did duty with the Metropolitan Police in the streets during the week following the collapse of the revolt.

The beginning made in this district on Monday by the attack on the defenceless Veterans' Corps was followed up by determined fighting throughout the week, and in no quarter of the city were the casualties heavier than those round about Mount Street, Clanwilliam Place and Sir Patrick Dun's Hospital. It was found necessary, so persistent was the fighting from the houses in Clanwilliam Place, to liberally bomb the insurgents out, and some idea of the severity of the contest may be formed by the record of cases suffering from gunshot wounds admitted to the Hospital during the week. One hundred and forty-two cases were treated, made up of 73 military and 69 civilians. Of these, 10 military and 11 civilians proved fatal.

Photo by T. W. Murphy.

TRINITY COLLEGE AND BANK OF IRELAND, DUBLIN.

The Pipers' Band of the Dublin University Officers' Training Corps.

The Morning Wash.—Troops in Trinity College.

Field Kitchens for the troops in Trinity College.

Photos by T. W. Murphy.

Outside the "Canteen."

Westland Row, as well as College Green, the task before the strategists was plainly one of no small magnitude. It was decided to place guards at the principal gates, and direct the attention of the main body upon holding the positions of the grounds most likely to be attacked from the Westland Row front, where the insurgents were in strength. The operations during Monday night were successful in checking an attack from this quarter, and on Tuesday with reinforcements it was possible to further strengthen the defences elsewhere. A position that in the hands of the rebels would constitute a very serious danger proved of inestimable worth, when the numbers of those holding it were so increased as to render its value for attack capable of realisation. Machine guns placed on the parapet and crack shots in favourable positions on the roof, broke up the effort of the rebels to keep up communication between their position at Cork Hill and the G.P.O. with Stephen's Green. Rebel sniping from the houses in Nassau Street and Fleet Street was kept within control, and it is largely due to the garrison of Trinity College that the entire sacking of Grafton Street by looters was prevented. This fact has been fully recognised by the merchants of the leading thoroughfare, and is being fittingly acknowledged.

Upon the arrival of troops from England, the University grounds were an admirable central depot, and proved of incalculable value. Here were accommodated a brigade of infantry, a battery of artillery and a regiment of cavalry. Our illustrations give some idea of the strange scenes within the sombre quadrangles.

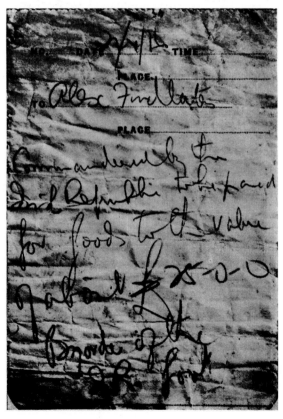

Something like a thousand men must have been on parade in the park of Trinity College on Saturday, May 20th, when General Sir John Maxwell, K.C.B., D.S.O., inspected the Officers' Training Corps of Dublin University and of the Royal College of Surgeons, several corps affiliated to the Irish Association of Volunteer Training Corps and St. John and Red Cross Ambulance units. General Maxwell, addressing the men, said that he was glad to have the opportunity of thanking the Provost and the officers and men of the University Officers' Training Corps for all they had done during recent events. It was thanks to their prompt assistance that that part of the city was kept from being ruined. He knew no more distasteful thing to men than to be called out to quell civil disturbances. The University Corps had most nobly responded to the call made upon them, and he thanked them very much indeed for their services in coming to the assistance of the military during the recent regrettable occurrences. Many of those whom he was addressing were unarmed, and, notwithstanding that, had exposed themselves most gallantly in the execution of their duty. It was impossible to allude to all classes who obeyed the call of duty, but the greater number of the citizens of Dublin did so, and did so nobly. To all of them he offered his deepest thanks.

A march past concluded the proceedings, and General Maxwell, standing by the Union Jack, gracefully acknowledged the salutes of the officers of the various Corps. Only the members of the University Corps carried arms. The Corps on parade were :—Dublin University O.T.C. and Royal College of Surgeons O.T.C.; Volunteer Training Corps, Rugby Union Corps, Veterans' Corps, Glasnevin Corps, D. Company (G.N.R., G.S. & W.R., North City, and South City), Greystones Corps, Bray Corps, St. John Ambulance and British Red Cross V.A.D.'s.

Indian students of the King's Inns, who performed ambulance work, paraded with the Rathmines unit.

Lower Sackville Street from the corner of Abbey Street, showing broken flag-post on G.P.O. from which Republican flag was flown.

were taken down into one of the cellars, and confined there for some time, while the front of the building was on fire. They tried to extinguish the fire, but failed in that. The rebels left some bombs outside the windows of the cell in which the soldiers were confined. The Sinn Fein men were ordered upstairs in order to get away from the fire, when the officer made a noise to attract their attention. They came back in response to the noise, and asked who was there. He answered by asking : " Are you going to leave us here to be burned like rats in a trap ? " The prisoners were marched out of the cell in single file, and sent upstairs. They were then conducted out into Henry Street, under an armed escort, and across to Moore Lane, where they were " halted " in the lane. They were then warned that they would have to run for their lives into Moore Street, where two of this officer's fellow-prisoners

On Wednesday, Thursday and Friday the fight for the General Post Office, the Headquarters of the Provisional Government, was pressed by the military with the greatest vigour ; artillery and machine guns placed near Trinity College sweeping Westmoreland Street, Sackville Street and D'Olier Street. On Friday night, the 28th, after three days' incessant bombardment with artillery and machine guns, fire broke out and rapidly spread from the G.P.O., ultimately enveloping the Hotel Metropole, the *Freeman's Journal* offices, Messrs. Eason's, and the entire block of adjoining buildings.

During the week's operations passages had been blasted from the Post Office through the adjoining buildings in Henry Street as far as the Coliseum Theatre. When the fire developed and the building became untenable, many of the insurgents found little difficulty in escaping in this way.

An Officer of the Royal Inniskilling Fusiliers was a prisoner in the General Post Office from Tuesday morning till Friday, having been captured by the rebels as he was on his way home through Sackville Street. He had as fellow-prisoners two other officers, either ten or twelve privates of different regiments, and a sergeant of the Dublin Metropolitan Police. The men in charge of the Post Office seemed to him to have been well supplied with ammunition and with food. On Friday night some of the prisoners

Photo by T. W. Murphy.

The Provisional Government
... TO THE ...
CITIZENS OF DUBLIN

The Provisional Government of the Irish Republic salutes the CITIZENS OF DUBLIN on the momentous occasion of the proclamation of a

Sovereign Independent Irish State

now in course of being established by Irishmen in Arms.

The Republican forces hold the lines taken up at Twelve noon on Easter Monday, and nowhere, despite fierce and almost continuous attacks of the British troops, have the lines been broken through. The country is rising in answer to Dublin's call, and the final achievement of Ireland's freedom is now, with God's help, only a matter of days. The valour, self sacrifice, and discipline of Irish men and women are about to win for our country a glorious place among the nations.

Ireland's honour has already been redeemed ; it remains to vindicate her wisdom and her self-control.

All citizens of Dublin who believe in the right of their Country to be free will give their allegiance and their loyal help to the Irish Republic. There is work for everyone ; for the men in the fighting line, and for the women in the provision of food and first aid. Every Irishman and Irishwoman worthy of the name will come forward to help their common country in this her supreme hour.

Able bodied Citizens can help by building barricades in the streets to oppose the advance of the British troops. The British troops have been firing on our women and on our Red Cross. On the other hand, Irish Regiments in the British Army have refused to act against their fellow countrymen.

The Provisional Government hopes that its supporters — which means the vast bulk of the people of Dublin — will preserve order and self-restraint. Such looting as has already occurred has been done by hangers-on of the British Army. Ireland must keep her new honour unsmirched.

We have lived to see an Irish Republic proclaimed. May we live to establish it firmly, and may our children and our children's children enjoy the happiness and prosperity which freedom will bring.

Signed on behalf of the Provisional Government,

P. H. PEARSE,

Commanding in Chief the Forces of the Irish Republic, and President of the Provisional Government.

The first Bulletin of the Commander-in-Chief of the Forces of the Irish Republic, issued from the Headquarters G.P.O.

After the Insurrection.—Interior General Post Office, Dublin.

came from the rebels on the opposite side of Sackville Street is not clear, but bullets went through the telephone box. After spending three hours in the box, two guards came down and conducted him to the staff diningroom on the top of the building for a meal. At night he was taken to a room overlooking the Metropole Hotel. There was no bedding whatever, and two guards kept the door with fixed bayonets, so that there was no sleep. On Tuesday, Wednesday and Thursday there was much firing, and the rebels were running all over the place. On Friday morning the roof of the Post Office caught fire. Downstairs the rebels had everything combustible smashed up ready to start a fire, and the cellars were packed with explosives. Bullets were then coming into the room where he and other captives, to the number of sixteen, were imprisoned.

Among the rebels were engineers, electricians, and experts of all kinds, including a man, undoubtedly from Berlin, who was an expert in regard to explosives. On Friday evening the prisoners were taken to a basement right below the building. Here were stores of gelignite, cordite, gun

were shot dead. He jumped into McGivney's shop, and lay there from seven o'clock on Friday evening till four next morning, when he found it necessary to make his escape from the fire which had seized that shop. As soon as he appeared in the street a fusilade was opened upon him from a barricade further down the street. He ran towards the Nelson Pillar and across to Cathedral Street, where, with some women who had come out of Hickey's warehouse, he took refuge in the Pro-Cathedral.

A series of extraordinary experiences and escapes fell to the lot of an officer of the 14th Royal Fusiliers, who was in Dublin on sick leave and was, of course, unarmed. He was also held a prisoner from Easter Monday to the following Friday, when he was given the choice of being shot immediately or running the gauntlet of soldiers' fire to draw it off the escaping rebels. After being searched for arms, the lieutenant was bound with wire obtained from the telephone box, and put into the box, which faced Nelson Pillar. By this time the public had scattered, and the officials, including some from other floors, had been marched out of the office with their hands above their heads. There was then a rush for the windows, which the rebels smashed with the butt-ends of their rifles and pikes. It was when the troop of Lancers charged that this prisoner had his first narrow escape from injury. Whether the Lancers fired or whether the shots

The reconstructed Public Office at the G.P.O. as it appeared before the revolt.

Photo by T. W. Murphy.

cotton, and dynamite—stacks of it. Men came down to the basement for bombs. The cellar was barricaded with boxes, and a light turned on to one of these revealed packages of gelignite. Bombs with fuses set were placed round the cellar by the rebels, who then left the prisoners in it. They were saved from a horrible death by a rebel lieutenant. In response to the calls of the prisoners the lieutenant said, " It's all right, boys," and took them up again into the burning building and out into the yard at the back. Their next move was through a corridor into a room at the back of the Post Office, where they were put under the charge of a woman in male attire, who flourished a loaded revolver. A little later the prisoners were led to Moore Lane and told to run. About 150 yards away were the troops with a machine gun, and they were firing down the lane. The officer referred to started to run, but he had not gone ten yards before the rebels shot him in the thigh, and shot a Dublin Fusilier fellow-prisoner through the head. By a rush some of the prisoners passed successfully the end of the lane, down which the troops fired the machine gun, and being called upon by more rebels to stop, darted down an alley way to their left, only to find themselves charging a British machine gun. Bullets spattered around them, but by a miracle they escaped injury, jumping a parapet a yard high. Running round yet another passage they found themselves in a courtyard at the back of Lipton's store, where the officer collapsed from his nerve-racking experience. He was carried on the back of a sergeant of the R.I.R. into a cellar.

Constable Dunphy (C Division), who was kept prisoner in the G.P.O. for six days, was saved from the molestation of some of the Citizen Army by The O'Rahilly, one of the rebel Commandants, who was very considerate towards the prisoners. Constable Dunphy and The O'Rahilly, after leaving the burning building, ran along towards Moore Lane, when they were sniped by the military. Dunphy was wounded ; the body of The O'Rahilly was found in Moore Lane.

The following is a copy of an order which was found on the body of The O'Rahilly. It was presumably written in the Post Office, and is dated April 28, the day before the Sinn Fein surrender. As it sets out the position from the insurgent point of view at this date, we quote the order in full :—

Army of the Irish Republic,
(Dublin Command),
Headquarters, April 28, 1916.

To Soldiers.

This is the fifth day of the establishment of the Irish Republic, and the flag of our country still floats from the most important buildings in Dublin, and is gallantly protected by the officers and Irish soldiers in arms throughout the country. Not a day passes without seeing fresh postings of Irish soldiers eager to do battle for the old cause. Despite the utmost vigilance of the enemy we have been able to get in information telling us how the manhood of Ireland, inspired by our splendid action, are gathering to offer up their lives if necessary in the same holy cause. We are here hemmed in, because the enemy feels that in this building is to be found the heart and inspiration of our great movement.

The O'Rahilly : a member of the Council and Captain in the Sinn Fein Volunteers.

Let us remind you what you have done. For the first time in 700 years the flag of a free Ireland floats triumphantly in Dublin City. The British Army, whose exploits we are for ever having dinned into our ears, which boasts of having stormed the Dardanelles and the German lines on the Marne, behind their artillery and machine guns, are afraid to advance to the attack or storm any position held by our forces. The slaughter they have suffered in the first few days has totally unnerved them, and they dare not attempt again an infantry attack on our position.

Our Commandants around us are holding their own. Commandant Daly's splendid exploit in capturing Linenhall Barracks we all know. You must know also that the whole population, both clergy and laity, of this district are united in his praises. Commandant MacDonagh is established in an impregnable position reaching from the walls of Dublin Castle to Redmond's Hill, and from Bishop Street to Stephen's Green.

(In Stephen's Green, Commandant —— holds the College of Surgeons, one side of the square, a portion of the other side, and dominates the whole Green and all its entrances and exits.)

Commandant de Valera stretches in a position from the Gas Works to Westland Row, holding Boland's Bakery, Boland's Mills, Dublin South-Eastern Railway Works, and dominating Merrion Square.

Commandant Kent holds the South Dublin Union and Guinness's Buildings to Marrowbone Lane, and controls James's Street and district. On two occasions the enemy effected a lodgment, and were driven out with great loss.

The men of North County Dublin are in the field, have occupied all the Police Barracks in the district, destroyed all the telegraph system on the Great Northern Railway up to Dundalk, and are operating against the trains of the Midland Great Western. Dundalk has sent 200 men to march upon Dublin, and in the other parts of the North our forces are active and growing. In Galway Captain ——, fresh after his escape from an Irish prison, is in the field with his men. Wexford and Wicklow are strong, and Cork and Kerry are equally acquitting themselves creditably. (We have every confidence that our Allies in Germany and kinsmen in America are straining every nerve to hasten matters on our behalf.)

As you know, I was wounded twice yesterday and am unable to move about, but have got my bed moved into the firing line, and with the assistance of your officers, will be just as useful to you as ever.

Courage, boys, we are winning, and in the hour of our victory let us not forget the splendid women who have everywhere stood by us and cheered us on. Never had man or woman a grander cause, never was a cause more grandly served.

(Signed), JAMES CONNOLLY,
Commandant-General, Dublin Division.

Photo by T. W. Murphy.

Corner of Bachelor's Walk and Lr. Sackville St. commanding O'Connell Bridge.

The premises of Messrs. Kelly & Son's gun and ammunition shop, which were strongly held and fortified, commanded the approaches to Sackville Street from the south side of the river. Upon the afternoon of Wednesday, after the military had cleared the neighbourhood of Brunswick Street and the district between that thoroughfare and the river, a nine-pounder was run into position at the back of Trinity College, and firing through D'Olier Street, raked Kelly's shop. The face of the building shown indicates the heavy firing to which it was subjected. It is interesting to find a place that stood so much of the shock of war being now devoted to the interests of the pipe of peace. The premises have now been taken over by Messrs. Kapp & Peterson.

On Wednesday the decision was reached by the military to bombard Liberty Hall with heavy artillery. Leaving Trinity College by the Brunswick Street gate, two eighteen-pounders were placed in position at Tara Street. Some difficulty was experienced in obtaining spade-hold for the trail of the guns in the paved street, but this was soon overcome, and many shells were thrown on Liberty Hall and Northumberland House, The bombardment was continued by the gunboat *Helga* from the river. Again difficulty was experienced, this time caused by the Loop Line Bridge, which intervenes between the river and the building. The ship's gunners dropped shells upon the roof, while machine guns were directed upon all avenues of escape, from vantage points at the Custom House.

An examination of the remains and debris of the interior of the building disclosed some interesting finds. The printing press and plant was intact, and numerous copies of the Official Proclamation of the Irish Republic were found, together with commissions appointing certain named persons to commands in the Citizen Army, and various other interesting documents.

Liberty Hall, Headquarters of the Citizen Army, after Bombardment.

These illustrations are of two stamps issued by the Sinn Fein organisation. The stamp with the cross design has been current for a considerable time, long, indeed, before the Sinn Fein developed militant tendencies. It was, frankly, a method of raising funds. These stamps were sold at 2/6 a gross, and the object was set forth in the *Sinn Fein* newspaper eight years ago as follows :—" It is to make the sign of Irish nationhood to the other nations that the stamp was designed. It is fulfilling that design as the Finnish stamp some years ago fulfilled a like design in calling the attention of the world to the fact that Finland was no province of Russia, but a nation despoiled, but separate and distinct, asserting its individuality and defending its liberties against foreign despotism." The stamp with the harp design is more modern and more interesting, inasmuch as it is printed in green and yellow on white— these being the Irish Republican colours. Its issue marks, therefore, a departure and an advance from the ideal of the original organisation to the ideal of the Citizen Army ; the fusion of these bearing fruit, of which the fire-scorched ruins in Dublin to-day are eloquent testimony. It is quite a mistake to regard either of these stamps as being intended as postage stamps ; they bear no postage value.

Photo by T. W. Murphy.

As Liberty Hall appeared after the opening of the European War. The offensive placard was subsequently removed by the Authorities.

In order to prevent the further slaughter of Dublin citizens, and in the hope of saving the lives of our followers now surrounded and hopelessly outnumbered, the members of the Provisional Government present at Head-Quarters have agreed to an unconditional surrender, and the Commandants of the various districts in the City and Country will order their commands to lay down arms.

P. H. Pearse
29th April 1916
3.45 p. m.

I agree to these conditions for the men only under my own Command in the Moore Street District and for the men in the Stephen's Green Command.

James Connolly
April 29/16

On consultation with Commandant Pearse and other officers I have decided to agree to unconditional surrender also.

Thomas MacDonagh.

The Surrender of Headquarters.

General " of the insurgent army in Dublin. The men under his immediate command, according to his surrender, appear to have been those in the Moore Street area, which may be taken to include the G.P.O., and also those at Stephen's Green.

These were in all probability mainly composed of men in the Citizen Army, a body called into being by James Larkin, following upon the labour disturbances in Dublin, 1913-14, and whose headquarters was Liberty Hall. When Larkin went to America James Connolly took up his responsibilities in Dublin, and appears to have succeeded in bringing about that fusion of the Citizen Army with the Sinn Fein Volunteers on the republican ideal, which has resulted in the revolt.

Connolly was a Cork man, the son of an artisan, and was about fifty years of age. Much of his youth was spent in Scotland, where he became identified with the Socialist movement, eventually becoming a paid Socialist lecturer, travelling over Scotland and England. He subsequently came to Belfast, taking charge of the Transport Workers' Union there, operating in close touch with James Larkin in Dublin.

Connolly was in control at the G.P.O. during the revolt, and was wounded there. He was tried by court-martial and sentenced to death. The sentence was carried out on May 12th, 1916.

THE FIRES.

Two and a half million pounds is mentioned by Captain Purcell, Chief of the Dublin Fire Brigade, as the approximate value of the buildings and stocks destroyed by fire during the rebellion. The total number of buildings destroyed in the Sackville Street area is clearly shown on the ground plan on the next page. Outside this area equally destructive fires occurred at Bridge Street, Usher's Quay, Harcourt Street, Linenhall Barracks, latterly the offices of the Army Pay Department. This latter fire involved portion of the ancient Linenhall, occupied by Messrs. Hugh Moore and Alexander, Limited, and also Messrs. Leckie & Co., of Bolton Street.

The first call came to the Brigade at 3.58 p.m. on Monday from the Ordnance Department at Island Bridge, reporting the fire at the Magazine Fort in the Phœnix Park. A detachment with a motor engine was sent from the Thomas Street Fire Station. At 10.6 p.m. the same day a box call came from the alarm at Nelson's Pillar, reporting the first of many fires in that area at the Cable Shoe Company's shop in Sackville Street. The Buckingham Street and Tara Street

Linenhall Barracks, used as the Army Pay Department—Remains after the fire.

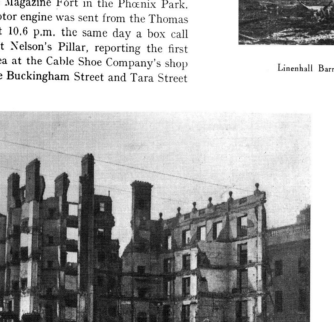

West side of Lr. Sackville Street, showing Ruins of Hotel Metropole.

sections succeeded by 11 o'clock in overcoming the flames there, when the services of the Brigade were necessary at the True-Form Boot Company's shop, also in Sackville Street. This fire was extinguished at 12.30 a.m. on Tuesday morning. Both shops had been looted before the fires occurred. At 12 o'clock on Tuesday, No. 4 Earl Street was reported burning. This was extinguished by 1 o'clock, and at 4.11 in the afternoon the great outbreak occurred at Lawrence's in Sackville Street. By hard work this—the largest conflagration that had yet occurred—was practically extinguished by a quarter past eight, a man and a woman being rescued by means of the fire escape from a top floor. At 12.59 on Wednesday, the 26th, a call came for Williams' Stores, at the back of Henry Street, which had been also looted at the time. The fire in this portion of the building was extinguished by 3 o'clock, but a fresh outbreak occurred in the front portion at 5.15 p.m., which was also extinguished.

The Harcourt Street outbreak occurred at 5 o'clock on the morning of Thursday, the 27th. By 7 o'clock this was extinguished, and the danger of spreading to the adjoining premises averted. The Linenhall fire was reported at 9.30 a.m.

Photos by Keogh Bros.

Plan showing the destroyed districts in the Sackville Street Area.

Published by courtesy of the Hibernian Fire and General Insurance Company.

The great outbreak in the Sackville Street area occurred at 12 noon on Thursday, commencing at the *Irish Times'* reserve printing works in Abbey Street. A barrier here conducted the flames to Wynn's Hotel on the other side of the street.

The military were now shelling this district, and the rifle volleying was of a terrific character, rendering it quite impossible for any attempt at operation on the part of the Brigade. The fires spread with incredible rapidity. All Thursday night this tremendous conflagration blazed, involving the entire block bound by Eden Quay, Sackville Street, Abbey Street, as far as Marlborough Street, and northwards the Sackville Street front as far as the scene of Tuesday's fire at Lawrence's.

Early on Friday morning, despite the immense risk, the Brigade turned out to see what could be done to prevent the spreading of the fires in the direction of North Earl Street, and this was fortunately done. While working on Friday in this district a call came to the Station from Bridge Street, and was attended to by the Thomas Street section. After several hours' work this fire was prevented from further spreading. The Buckingham Street section attended another

Eden Quay Area—After the Fires

The Linotype room in the "Freeman's Journal" office, Princes Street, after the fire.

call from Harcourt Street, where a dwellinghouse was ablaze. By 6 o'clock this was extinguished.

At 3.40 p.m. on Saturday word was conveyed by the military that the leaders of the rebels were in custody, and that military operations in Sackville Street endangering the lives of the firemen would cease. The whole force of the Brigade was immediately turned out. By that time the Post Office was gone; the Hotel Metropole and Eason's were burning fiercely. Two motor engines were started on O'Connell Bridge lifting water from the Liffey with four lines of delivery hose, and six other lines served from hydrants were all soon at work. After little more than half an hour's work Captain Purcell had evidence that his firemen were being deliberately sniped; men on the ladders felt the bullets fly about them, the escapes and engines being hit several times. Nothing remained but to call the men off and get them back to the stations. Injury to the aerial ladders was discovered on examination, six bullets having cut through the steel tubes at various places.

Photos by T. W. Murphy.

An urgent call coming from Marlborough Street reported serious developments imminent in the north side of North Earl Street likely to involve large warehouses situated there. Captain Purcell, after the dangerous experience in Sackville Street, yet impressed with the gravity of the new situation, called for volunteers. Lieutenant Meyers and four men immediately proceeded to the locality indicated, and were successful in limiting the fire and preventing further harm. The alarm was now received that Jervis Street Hospital was in imminent danger of becoming ignited by the burning debris falling upon its roof and outbuildings. To the firemen's credit, they one and all declared their willingness to risk the bullets if it were a question of saving the Hospital and its helpless inmates. Captain Purcell sought the assistance of the brigades of Power's Distillery and Guinness's Brewery, which was readily given. During the whole of Saturday night all worked with a will; success crowned their efforts, and the Hospital was saved. This arduous night's work concluded a memorable week's operations, and closed, save for occasional re-kindlings, the most appalling and devastating fires that have ever occurred within living memory in the city.

Ruins in Eden Quay. The fall of a dangerous building.

Sackville Street from Eden Quay to Abbey Street. Outer Walls of D.B.C: Restaurant still standing.

From Monday, 1st May, it was possible for those who could gain admittance within the military cordon to move about and view the ruins in the Sackville Street area. Stupefaction was widespread at the scenes of desolation. Here and there a cloud of smoke rose from smouldering heaps of ruins. Only a few blackened walls and gaunt chimney stacks remained on one side from Nelson's Pillar to O'Connell Bridge. The General Post Office was a mere shell, the interior roofless, a mass of smouldering debris; and from there to Abbey Street was entirely destroyed. Eden Quay, Abbey Street, Henry Street alike totally destroyed. The imagination staggers at the contemplation of such masses of wreckage. The prevailing impression on the spectator is that of contemplating a picture of some war-worn town, maybe in France or Flanders, presented with an overpowering and horrible realism.

This feeling was accentuated by the frequent passage of Ambulances to and fro, and the presence of Red Cross Nurses moving about in their striking uniform, within call for their merciful service when some poor bruised body is found amid the piles of wreckage.

Photos by T. W. Murphy.

Coliseum Theatre, front entrance at Henry St.

Ruins of the Coliseum Theatre.—View from the Stage.

RESCUE FROM THE RUINS OF THE COLISEUM THEATRE.

On Wednesday morning, 3rd May, between 10 and 11 o'clock, two soldiers named Sergeant Henry, of the School of Musketry, Dollymount Camp, and Private James Doyle, Royal Irish Regiment, Beggar's Bush Barracks, were discovered among the ruins of the Coliseum Theatre in Henry Street. It appears that these two men were among the military prisoners held in the G.P.O. When the progressing fire in that building made the place a veritable inferno, they were turned out into the bullet-swept streets. They made their way to the Theatre, and took safety in the Coliseum buildings, and being under the impression that firing was still going on, remained in the ruins until, fortunately, discovered as stated. They had no food of any sort since the previous Friday, and the wonder is that, in the precarious and dangerous position they found themselves in, they were able to retain any strength.

They were both conveyed to the Central Police Station, and were subsequently taken away in a military van. They walked from the station to the van actively, and beyond showing a dishevelled appearance were seemingly in good spirits.

Photos by T. W. Murphy.

Sandbag defences placed across the road at the Railway Bridge at Clontarf.

Richmond Barracks used as a Detention Prison.

Annesley Bridge was seized on Monday afternoon, a strong guard being mounted in the Dublin and Wicklow Manure Company's Offices. Similarly, Ballybough Bridge and adjoining houses were garrisoned ; motor cars and lorries seized from parties passing were made use of to barricade the roads, and foot passengers were only permitted to pass these points upon answering questions put to them to the satisfaction of the insurgent sentry on duty, searching being in some cases resorted to.

Attempts were made on Tuesday to blow up the Great Northern Railway line where it crosses the new Fairview Park. This was apparently unsuccessful. The arrival of the military on Wednesday morning altered the condition of affairs ; a sharp engagement ending the occupation of Annesley Bridge by the insurgents. A detachment of infantry with a machine gun was mounted on the railway bridge near Howth Road, and working up the railway line towards Amiens Street Station soon had it securely in their possession.

On Saturday a rumour gained currency that insurgent reinforcements were expected from the northern district, and military preparations were quickly got under way. A strong party of voluntary workers were got together, and the erection of sandbag defences was quickly made at two points on the main road, with machine guns mounted. In this district towards the end of the week the food question threatened to become disturbing. A Citizens' Committee was formed, under the chairmanship of Alderman Jas. Moran, and arrangements were made for a supply of grocery provisions from Drogheda and bread from Belfast brought down by special trains. Willing volunteers assisted in the distribution of these, and what might have proved a serious shortage of food was averted.

Pho'os by J. W. Murp y.

The last Act—Prisoners being conveyed to the boats for deportation.

The march past of the British Red Cross Voluntary Aid Detachment. at the Review of Volunteers in Trinity College.

No record of the lamentable proceedings during Easter week in Dublin would be complete without mention of the merciful and heroic work of rescue and aid for the wounded, often carried out under conditions of the greatest risk and danger. Fortunately, voluntary aid in Dublin has, since the outbreak of the European War, been brought to a high pitch of organisation and efficiency. The British Red Cross detachments and the St. John Ambulance Brigade form an enthusiastic army of voluntary nurses and stretcher-bearers, whose services proved simply invaluable. The scheme of motor ambulances, so highly organised by the Irish Automobile Club, and which has done such successful service in the transport of wounded soldiers of war from the hospital ships, was made fully available, and from the demands made upon them in this emergency one trembles to think what would have happened if such an event had occurred in different circumstances. In addition to the regular hospitals in the city, which were, of course, pressed to their uttermost limits, auxiliary hospitals were improvised, and staffs got together with full equipment in an incredibly short space of time. There were over 600 men and women engaged in this noble and gallant work during the rebellion. There are very many cases of outstanding heroism recorded on the part of stretcher-bearers, both male and female, and of those in charge of ambulance vehicles. There are also many in which sheer human pity for the suffering wounded elevated the spectators to a condition where consciousness of personal risk was utterly forgotten. Of such a character was the incident during the attack on the

Sherwood Foresters at Clanwilliam Place, when a young girl seeing the soldiers fall on Mount Street Bridge under the merciless hail of bullets, rushed out from the crowd, and notwithstanding the heavy firing endeavoured to carry a wounded man to a place of safety. This she was unable to do, but she stood over him with her hands up until help came, when he was taken to the Nurses' Home in Mount Street.

Less sensationally striking, but none the less merciful and heroic, was the work done in the regular city hospitals. At the Castle Red Cross Hospital during the week one hundred and eighteen wounded soldiers, thirty-four insurgents, twenty civilians and two policemen were treated ; thirty-six deaths occurred. At Jervis Street Hospital upwards of four hundred cases were attended to. At Steevens' Hospital one hundred and five cases were seen in the accident room. Royal City of Dublin Hospital, two hundred cases, of whom one hundred and forty-seven were detained, seventeen died in hospital, fourteen dying or dead on arrival. Adelaide Hospital, seventy-five cases and four deaths, and five admitted in a dying state. Richmond Hospital, one hundred and fifty cases, forty detained, seventeen dying or dead on arrival. The Mater Hospital, over four hundred cases, eighty-six detained, twenty-nine deaths. Holles Street Hospital, out of forty-two cases thirty were detained, seven deaths. At Mercer's Hospital, two hundred and fifty-four cases of gunshot were treated, of which fifty were detained, and twenty-five deaths. St. Vincent's Hospital, fifty cases, five deaths. King George's Military Hospital, about one hundred cases.

Sisters of Charity feeding hungry boys during the revolt.

Photos by College Studios and T. W. Murphy.

Under the presidency of Sir Henry A. Robinson, Vice-President of the Local Government Board, a Committee to superintend food supplies was appointed. The machinery of the Society of St. Vincent de Paul was availed of to reach necessitous cases in the city with direct free distribution of food. Local Relief Committees dealt with such needs in the townships and more outlying districts. The organisation and officers of the Ministry of Munitions and the Department of Recruiting, with telephone communication at certain points, arranged for assisting traders to obtain supplies, and where necessary provided military transport. Arrangements were also made for supplies to the various institutions, containing in many cases a large number of helpless inmates.

The Mansion House was thrown open by the Lord Mayor (Councillor Gallagher) to refugees deprived in many cases by fire of the shelter of their own houses, in others prevented from reaching their humble homes through the bullet-swept streets. The Lord Mayor personally interested himself in work of the utmost importance and urgency, in arranging for and supervising the burial of the dead from hospitals and various districts. This work was fraught in many cases with serious difficulty ; vans and vehicles had to be borrowed ; coffins to the extent necessary were impossible to obtain. In some cases arrangements for temporary interment had to be made, and passage through the military cordons upon these sad journeys could, in the circumstances, only be arranged for by some such person in authority. Great assistance is said to have been given to his Lordship by Mr. O'Connell Fitzsimons, Superintendent of the City Markets and Commandant of the Pembroke detachment of the British Red Cross Society. Mr. Fitzsimons conveyed numerous bodies to the various cemeteries in a van for burial.

The ruins of Messrs. Eason & Sons' Premises, in Mid. Abbey St.

General Sir John Maxwell conveyed to the doctors, nurses and ambulance helpers generally his appreciation of their services during the revolt in the following order, which was issued on the 7th May :—

"Headquarters, Irish Command, Parkgate, Dublin, 7th May, 1916. I desire to express my sincere appreciation of the services rendered during the recent disturbances in Dublin by the medical, surgical and nursing staffs of many of the city hospitals, and in particular of the gallantry shown by those nurses who exposed themselves to a heavy fire in attending to and removing the wounded. Also to the members of the Red Cross and St. John Ambulance Societies, and the many medical men and private individuals who gave assistance in attending to the wounded or placed their houses at the disposal of the military for use as dressing stations. In numerous instances these services were rendered at considerable personal risk and under circumstances reflecting the greatest credit on those engaged in them. (Signed), J. G. Maxwell, General, Commanding-in-Chief the Forces in Ireland."

Nuns distributing food to the necessitous poor.

Photos by T. W. Murphy.

Inspection of Motor Ambulances at the Royal Barracks, May 27th.

General Sir John Maxwell has a few words for each of the drivers and orderlies.

A type of Armoured Car familiar in the Dublin Streets.

An Armoured Motor Waggon used in the revolt, built in eight hours in one of the Dublin Engineering Yards

Photos by T. W. Murphy.

THE LOOTING.

A walk through the central portions of the city on Easter Tuesday would hardly strike one as being either the time or the place for moralising. Yet Sackville Street—quite safe in the forenoon of that day—to anyone given to reflection, presented a spectacle and a condition of things irresistibly interesting. Here, in the course of a few hours, constituted authority was boldly challenged and for the time overthrown. The feeling was a novel one. In the principal street of the capital of the country, with warehouses crammed on every side with the most valuable stocks that the city affords, neither policeman nor soldier, nor tram nor other vehicle ; only a street full of sightseers with something of a holiday air, and frequent houses with barricaded windows and grim, silent men leaning on them within, waiting with rifles in their hands for the attack that one felt must be in preparation, and would be relentless when it came.

At the Post Office men lounged at the windows that were stuffed with mail bags, some smoking, some munching rations from their shoulder-slung haversacks, and others exchanging a few hurried words with women folk on the footway—anxious wives or mothers or sweethearts. Two slender strands of barbed wire streeled slackly across the street, and a boy, looking not more than sixteen years old, with a shot gun, stood near them in the centre. On one side a huge plate-glass window was smashed in to afford means of reaching a pillar inside the window, round and round which the barbed wire was coiled, from whence it crossed to the corner of the Hotel Metropole. Barbed wire is an unfriendly, menacing and ugly thing : one resents coming upon it on a country ramble even in some rustic lane. Here in Sackville Street, sprawling through that ruptured window, it seemed a hideous and challenging enormity. The luxuriously plush-covered pillar, gashed and torn with it, seemed to shriek that red ruin was afoot. Near at hand a lad emerged from a looted hat shop, stripped of the last article of men's headgear. All he could find, apparently, was a leather tall-hat case and a huge footman's umbrella. In some bewilderment he examined the hat case. The shape seemed familiar, but how was he to wear it ? Presently it occurred to him to rip the lid off, and stuffing it nearly full of waste paper he jammed it on his head, and opening the enormous umbrella he swaggered off to the delighted shrieks of a crowd of ragged urchins about him. A few yards further on was an aged and anxious-eyed woman, with all a mother's premonition of coming danger, her hands on the shoulders of a young fellow wearing a bandolier, pleading unavailingly with him to come home with her and leave it all behind. Near by dead, still lay in the street two of the troopers' horses, mute witnesses of the affray with the Lancers on Monday. Surely the fair fabric of civilisation hangs by a slender thread. Here it had fallen at our feet, all rumpled—anyhow !

Of course, much of the looting must have been of a sordid and desperate character. That was the night work, when darkness covered and hid the evil. The looting that met the eye in daytime—open and unashamed, as a great deal of it was—seemed to be carried out more in the spirit of the childish careless souvenir hunter than that of the prowling thief. One was impressed with the utter uselessness to the class that carried them of most of the articles in their possession. There was indeed little that was furtive and nothing of fear in the manner of their bearing. That this light-hearted spirit was prevalent in daytime at all events, is shown by the fact that the lollypop shops were the first to go. Boot shops seem also to have been quite irresistible. Lawrence's toyshop provided a great deal of delight to the gamin order, and despite the grimness of the situation, some amusement to the onlookers. A frantic race took place in the lower end of Abbey Street, for instance, between a barefoot boy on a tricycle motor car, value for at least a few pounds, and a small boy on foot dragging an elephant bigger than himself, by the ear. In Talbot Street a boy arrayed in a suit many sizes too big for him, and with the price label still on the breast of the coat, was wielding a fine golf driver against a tennis ball. After each stroke he took from his pocket an expensive pair of binoculars and languidly surveyed the course of the shot. At Manfield's boot establishment a woman left the shop and deposited an apron load of boots on the footpath. She went back for more, and on returning found that the original supply had disappeared. Her indignation was fierce and eloquent. She denounced the crowd jointly and severally, and having exhausted her vituperation on them, bitterly railed at the absence of the police and their failure to protect her property.

During the looting of a house furnishing shop in Camden Street an elderly woman emerged from the premises staggering beneath a heavy armchair. "Here, Mary, hold that," she said to a young girl, apparently her daughter, "till I go back and get the match of it."

A pair of factory girls, with work-a-day shawls over their heads, sauntered down Britain Street arm in arm, each carrying an expensive tennis racquet, looking as if they were discussing the pros and cons of a game of ladies singles just contested in the Rotunda Gardens.

One cannot find much in the way of an attractive excuse for such offences against the accepted laws of "meum and tuum" as the possession in a tenement dwelling of six sacks of flour and two bags of sugar—not uncommon in the cases tried before the looting Court.

The opening of Easter week had indeed something in it of the blending of the smile and the tear, so characteristic of the peculiar genius of Dublin. While Comedy shook his bells and bauble, the sombre skirts of Tragedy rustled on the threshold.

J. W. M.

* * * * * *

"A battery of artillery couldn't stop that," said a passer-by noticing a carriage and pair with wedding favours at the horses' heads, waiting at the door of a well-known Clontarf Church ; a marriage ceremony taking place within while the rifles and machine guns rattled furiously from the railway bridge at hand and the rebels at Croydon Park.

* * * * * *

"Queer people, you Irish," remarked a Sherwood Forester during the rebellion ; "some of you shoot us in the back while others stuff us with refreshment and smother us with kindness."

REBEL LEADERS SURRENDER.

THREE PRINCIPALS TRIED AND SHOT.

OTHERS ARRESTED & HELD FOR TRIAL UNCONDITIONALLY.

SERIOUS FIGHTING ALL ROUND THE CITY

HEAVY CASUALTIES IN DEAD AND WOUNDED.

CENTRE OF DUBLIN DEVASTATED BY FIRE; PALATIAL BUILDINGS IN ASHES.

The Sinn Fein insurrection, which broke out in Dublin City, on Easter Monday, at noon, has been effectively quelled.

The positions of vantage which the rebels took up in various parts of the city were reduced, and the leaders unconditionally surrendered.

Thomas J. Clarke, P. H. Pearse, and Thomas Macdonagh, three of the signatories to the poster proclaiming an Irish Republic, have been tried by court-martial and shot. The dead body of The O'Rahilly was found in Moore lane, adjacent to the G.P.O. James Connolly, Larkin's chief lieutenant, is wounded and a prisoner. F. Sheehy Skeffington has been shot.

The centre of the city has suffered severely from fire. The beautiful shops on one of the finest thoroughfares in Europe, Lr. O'Connell street, are a shapeless mass of ruins, while most of Henry street, Middle Abbey street, Earl street, and Prince's street and Eden quay, is in a similar condition.

No approximate estimate even of the casualties suffered by the military, the rebels, and civilians is available, but the number of deaths is large, and the people injured very numerous.

Portion of the Post Office was saved from the flames.

PANDEMONIUM RENEWED.

There was a lull in the fighting from 4 in the afternoon up to 7 o'clock, when the pandemonium broke out afresh, and the horror of the whole scene was added to when darkness fell, and the centre of the distracted city, viewed from the suburbs, seemed to be one mass of flames. The suburbs were lighted up by the glare as if it were noonday.

Up to eleven o'clock on Friday morning there was a lull in the firing, when activities were again resumed in the Clontarf district. The military Red Cross ambulance became busy about noon. The lines were extended further out in the city, and the sentries had in many cases to fire over the heads of the people to get them to disperse. All night long rifle and machine gun fire resounded in the Drumcondra district, and a civilian standing outside his home in Hollybank road received a bullet wound in the leg. The city was again one mass of flames at night.

NEARING THE END.

On the morning of Saturday the military had all but cleared the city of the insurgents. Thousands of people in the suburbs who were unable to obtain bread during the night were allowed to pass through the military lines to the city bakeries. About thirty prisoners, mostly youths, were surrounded by a cordon of soldiers with fixed bayonets at Parnell Monument, and were removed about midday. On Saturday afternoon it was rumoured that P. H. Pearse, of St. Enda's College, Rathfarnham, had surrendered on behalf of the insurgents at the Headquarters of the Military Command at Parkgate street. When the firing ceased for several hours in the afternoon credence was given to the statement freely circulated that at last the Volunteers had given in. About eight o'clock, however, the big guns again shrieked forth their message of death. The snipers in the suburbs resumed their isolated firing, and all hopes of a conclusion of the ghastly fight were instantly abandoned. Late that night or in the small hours of Sunday morning the insurgents in the G.P.O. surrendered to Sir John Maxwell. It became officially known on Saturday afternoon that practically all the insurgents, including Mr. Pearse had surrendered unconditionally, and this relieved anxiety to a considerable extent.

CHURCH BELLS SILENT.

Church bells were silent on the North side on Sunday evening, and the only sounds were the rifle shots and the machine gun fire. Heavy cannonading proceeded from the direction of Swords, and at three o'clock in the evening seven hundred Lancers and Hussars, with machine

OFFICIAL.

REVOLUTIONARY LEADERS

THREE TRIED AND SHOT.

PEARSE, CLARKE, AND MACDONAGH

"Three signatories of the notice proclaiming the Irish Republic, P. H. Pearse, T. Macdonagh, and T. J. Clarke, have been tried by Field General Court Martial and sentenced to death. The sentences having been duly confirmed, the three above-mentioned men were shot this (Wednesday) morning. The trial of further prisoners is proceeding.

"Yesterday there were still some small disturbances in the South and West of Ireland, in which some casualties have occurred. The rest of Ireland is reported quiet.

"Larne has been added to the list of ports from which passengers may leave Ireland.

"Until further notice no aliens will be allowed to land in Ireland unless in possession of a permit which can be obtained from the Military Permit Officer, 19 Bedford Square, London, or from the Military Control Officer, Room 347, Royal Liver Buildings, Liverpool.

"All persons who intend to travel between England and Ireland should be in possession of papers proving their identity."

Joseph Plunkett, and Thomas MacDonagh.

Eoin McNeill, Commandant of the Irish Volunteers, did not sign it, and the inference drawn was that he did not approve of the proceedings.

When the squadron of Lancers appeared in O'Connell street on Easter Monday they were immediately fired on from the top of the G.P.O., and two men and two horses were killed. The dead horses lay in the street during the afternoon.

Some time before the military appeared in the street a Howth tram was held up at the corner of Earl street, and an attempt was made, by placing two bombs beneath it, to throw it off the line. The sound of an explosion was deafening. Crowds ran helter skelter in all directions out of O'Connell street, and many were knocked down and trampled on in the rush. The tram, however, remained immovable, and throughout the evening was in position on the line.

STRATEGIC POINTS SEIZED.

The cavalry again formed up in Parnell street with their lances at the present. The colonel in charge kept his men

the Citizen Army entered the precincts of Dublin Castle. A policeman at the Upper Castle Gate was shot dead, and some of the men scaled the gates. At the same time armed men forced their way into the City Hall, and got out on the roof, whence they commanded the main entrance to the Castle. They also took possession of the Dublin "Daily Express" newspaper office, and from the roof and windows of this they guarded the approaches—Dame street, Castle street, and Cork Hill—to the Upper Castle Yard.

The attack was absolutely unexpected. Comparatively few people were in the vicinity at the time, and the attacking party assembled quietly within a few minutes—some on foot, and others on bicycles, and all armed with rifles.

At 12.20 crowds of men, women and children collected along the footways, when suddenly a fusillade of about a dozen rifle shots was fired from the roof of the City Hall down Parliament street, the stone balustrade on the flat roof being used for fire embrasures.

A CIVILIAN SHOT.

MY UNCLE
By Michael Collins

continued from page 22

After this, yet another abortive rising, Collins who was now 26 was incarcerated in the grounds of the Rotunda Hospital, which was even then, and still is, one of the most famous Maternity Hospitals, not only in Ireland, but perhaps in the world. Collins was there for a couple of weeks. His second Cousin Nancy O'Brien had in the meantime been transferred back to Dublin on promotion. When she found that the prisoners were going to be shipped from Dublin Docks to Frongoch prison, to Brixton and other Jails, she thought she would seek him out on their way down the Quays to Alexander Basin from where the ships would depart.

In her own words, "There was never a more dejected, down-hearted and dispirited looking group of men". They were pelted with rotten eggs and tomatoes by the women of Dublin City. Understandably so, for there was no employment for them in the Dublin of the time, and they were dependent on the money coming back from the Front from their husbands and sons fighting with the British Army. They regarded these youngsters as a crowd of pups.

Through all the despondency and the dejection she heard the familiar whistling of *The Banks of My Own Lovely Lee*. She found Michael ebullient, and full of the joys of Spring. "What has you so good humored? " she asked Michael as she walked alongside him.

"I have twelve names here Nancy and after six weeks I know we'll be ready for the next round. And we will win the next round with men of integrity and commitment".

"Michael" she said, "you'll soon be 26 and should you not be thinking of your future?. Will you be able to get back into the Civil Service?" He put his arm around her and said "Come here Nancy girl, where can you do better conceptual thinking than in the grounds of the Rotunda Maternity Hospital?"!.

These were prophetic words and they were to become reality in a very short while. As he was marched down the Quays he thought of the fiasco of the GPO Rising and was determined that next time things would be planned differently. There would be no sitting target, no static positions where the Helga could come up the Liffey and blast the hell out of us.

"We were like lambs to the slaughter. 'Noble' they called it. 'Shameful' I'd call it". Surely by this stage of the twentieth century, these true hearted genuine Irishmen should have learned from the mistakes of the past and ensured that they would never find themselves in such a position again.

On his release from Frongoch prison he began collecting men and women for his Movement. Collins went for four weeks to Southhampton, Manchester and Liverpool. All over Dublin City he met the navvies, the dockers, the sailors, the barmen, and particularly the dairymen and the fruit sellers because these people in a natural situation would arouse no suspicion with the British during their daily rounds selling their fruit and vegetables in Moore Street and other places.

Collins met the vast majority of this disparate group of people once only.

I spoke to several of them who remember their meeting as if it was yesterday, still remembering the impact of that meeting which showed his power and determination, and the conviction that he could win the vital necessity of confidentiality.

"If you get them over the Irish sea I'll have them, (i.e., guns) taken from you by safe men to safe houses and you will never be under suspicion", he told the men working on the cross-channel boats.

He established for himself around the perimeter of Dublin City seven or eight bolt holes where he could go when under extreme pressure.

The British were beginning to see that the movement was gathering momentum and for the entire duration of the War of Independence he was convinced that the best form of disguise was none at all. It is now hard to imagine that Collins fought against the might of the Empire of Britain from a bicycle as he cycled from one of these bolt holes to another.

There was a price of £10,000 on his head, and where the average worker's wage in those years was two pounds, two shillings a week, not one Irish Citizen harboured the thought of betraying this young West Cork man who was becoming the main figure of hope of this fight.

Dan Breen had set the ball rolling with the Soloheadbeg ambush in Co. Tipperary on 21st. January 1919 along with his comrades Sean Treacy, Seamus Robinson, Sean Hogan, Tim Crowe, Patrick O'Dwyer, Michael Ryan, Patrick McCormack and Jack O'Mara.

SOLOHEADBEG REMEMBERED

(Above) These photos taken by the editor in 1959 include veterans of the War of Independence as they marched to their former comrade Sean Treacy's grave in Kilfeacle cemetery.

(Right) Treacy's companion Dan Breen, (white hair, front row) stood by his graveside and remembered Soloheadbeg.

Dan came up to Dublin to report to Collins, his Commander-in-Chief. Ironically at that time Collins' working day was 5am to midnight, and as my mother said, with a degree of irony, "He had fixed the appointment for Dan for 5am, which would be the nearer the time that Dan would be going to bed never mind coming to an appointment!.

I visited Dan Breen, who later became a T.D., many a time myself during the last few years of his life, - most of which was spent in the Brothers of St. John of God in Kilcroney, and learned an invaluable amount of Irish History from him. Those who may have seen him on Telefis Eireann in its early years may recall hearing Maurice O'Doherty trying to get some criticisms out of Dan about Collins, and when asked towards the end of the interview what he thought of Collins, that raw faced powerful man looked into the television camera and without any embarrassment said "I loved him".

Breen told me himself, he went into that meeting with Collins in 1919 full of the spirit of Solohead at 5 o'clock in the morning and Collins said to him, "I have a quarter of an hour left so let's get down to business". "I want to tell you Comdt. Breen that your command is at risk. You broke two of my orders at that ambush". And Dan told me he was truly astonished. "You had a married man in the ambush" he said "and you as Commander showed yourself flamboyantly and ostentatiously to the end".

Dan, the raw faced Tipperary man said, "Christ Mick, what are those bloody words you've said"? "They're criticisms, and they shouldn't have happened". Dan was off his guard and downhearted, but before he knew where he was, Collins was across the desk and having grabbed him by the shoulders they ended up grovelling on the flat of his back on the floor where they wrestled for a few minutes!.

Dan then told him how on many a night on the Galtees he would never have gotten through without a plug of tobacco and a small Jameson.

Dan Breen was asked by Collins nine months later to do a special task which needed a special man. He was summoned to Dublin and Michael detailed what he wanted done. "You will be accompanied by a man who knows Dublin like the back of his hand", he said. They found themselves up in the Drumcondra area at 2am in the morning with the British Army all around and his companion said, "Don't worry Dan, we can always escape through Professor Carolan's rear garden across the wall and we'll be on a back road then and we'll get away safely".

They had forgotten that Professor Carolan had built a glass house under the bedroom window and, as Breen told me, he jumped straight through it with his hat on !. Dan was incarcerated in the Mater Hospital where he told me he was so injured that he had no interest at that moment in the future of Ireland, and couldn't care less what happened to Collins in the fight. In his own words; "I was falling into a broken sleep when at 6:30am a little biteen of a nurse came in and said;

"And how are we this morning Mr. Breen ?". "I told her" he said, "in non-dictionary language how I was and hoped she was somewhat better". "She plumped up my pillows. I was now awake and I saw there were two British Soldiers on each door of the ward. She was kind, even though I didn't appreciate it at the time. She said to me, 'Take that medicine under the pillow when I leave, Mr. Breen".

Breen put his hand under the pillow and he told me with tears in his eyes "God dammit Michael, under that pillow was the Plug of Mick McQuaid and a baby Jameson, -the two things I needed most". I relate this incident to illustrate how, for Michael Collins, his men and women were first in his thoughts and in that extraordinary organisational ability that beat the British, nothing was left out. For him, no task was too big or too little. Here was a man taking on the might of the Empire and yet he recorded in his mind what Dan would most appreciate at this time. No wonder Dan loved him and though they differed subsequently, Breen spoke with extraordinary clarity and driving conviction of what a tragedy Collins' death was to the Nation.

Curfew was nine o'clock but Collins didn't know the meaning of curfew. He was running this war from 5 in the morning 'till midnight and he knew that the most vital ingredient in the war with the British was to beat them to the punch. Therefore the only successful revolutionary in Irish history realised that even if he was to have a chance to win, he must get inside the thought process of the British.

In Neil Jordan's epic movie *Michael Collins*, the main person in Dublin Castle is depicted as Eamon Broy. The fact is that the main man in the Castle was the great and brave Dave Nelligan who wrote those absorbing articles 30 years later in the *Evening Herald* called *The Spy in the Castle* detailing what life in the Castle was like then. He, Broy, Kavanagh from Kilmacow in Co. Kilkenny and James McNamara laid their individual collective lives on the line every day they went into that Castle and with every document they got out safely to Collins. It is a fact that right through that vital period of 1919 and early 1920 the documents of instruction to every army and barracks in Ireland were in the hands of Collins before the officers and the head constables in those barracks ever got them.

That was the tremendous organisation, and clear thinking of an extraordinary mind that finished its formal education at 12 years of age but used every minute and hour of each day to convert the dream of a young fellow into the reality of freedom that you and I enjoy to-day.

In 1919 Mr. de Valera decided that, as an American citizen, he would gain entry to President Wilson and would have an influence on America in this fight for freedom. de Valera was married with a young family and it is amazing that he spent seventeen months in the United States. During all that period, terrifying warfare was going on back home, where the British, with an eye on world public opinion, could not have their armies carry out despicable acts to beat down this dedicated young bunch of men who were taking on the might of the great British Empire.

However, they brought over the "Auxies" and the Black and Tans, and the war, in which Collins' over-riding determination was that the least possible number should be killed, turned dirty. Villages, towns, localities were shot up, burned and brutalised. Collins met fire with fire. The ambushes continued and grew more successful.

The tide was beginning to turn. The vast majority of the people were fighting and following the instructions of this man they idolised because of what they knew were his characteristics. Each of them were men and women who were not expendable. Nobody should be put at risk but nobody demurred from the ultimate sacrifice that was asked of them to ensure that the cap-touching, forelock tipping of centuries and the castles and stately homes that were a reminder to boys and girls that we were a slave nation would be changed forever. That would not be the lot of the Irish people ever again, and therefore there was this tremendous will to win. Collins went from post to post, meeting the problems of the day, and every commander, no matter how small the unit was throughout the entire island knew that if there was a problem, "Get to Mick, and he'll get it done".

The British were now desperately worried as to how they could cope with these will-o-the-wisps who would hit them and then vanish. In late 1919, Nancy O'Brien whom I mentioned earlier, had got rapid promotion in the Post Office. She was sitting in her office when she was sent for by the head of the British Post Office,- the civilian side of British rule in Ireland, The Hon. James McMahon.

He said to her, "We are aware of your dedication and your work". "I must say to you", he said, "that there's a young man from your own country who like all of the idiots in century after century would look at the might of the British Empire and think they could take it on. Michael Collins is his name".

"Oh! Yes!" she said, "I've heard of him".

"That man" he said " will fail inevitably like all those damn fools before him. To get to the point Miss O'Brien", he said "We must admit he has the military information even before the officers to which it is sent. Whitehall is now so worried that they are going to send the vital civilian information necessary for running this outpost of our Empire in code, and we have decided, because of your dedication and your lack of interest in this person that you will be the person to decode all of these messages".

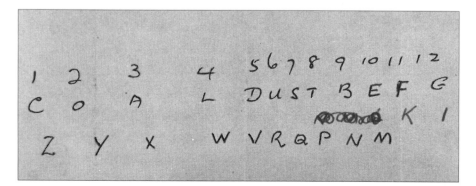

Nancy O'Brien, the writer's mother who daily risked her life by smuggling out to General Collins the ever changing codes on scraps of paper which she carried folded in her hair.

Below left is an actual sample.

Nancy O'Brien was shocked to say the least and having got the instructions that it would start from the coming Wednesday, she contacted Joe McGrath and said, "I need to see Mick". Joe McGrath knew that Nancy O'Brien would not look for Mick unless something important was on. He got back to her, "Mick will meet you in Vaughan's Hotel at 8 o' clock tonight". "He'd better be on time" said Nancy O' Brien, "because the curfew is 9 o'clock and as a loyal servant of the British Empire and I must be at home in my bed myself by then!"

She went to Vaughan's Hotel at 8 o'clock, where she recognised, - swinging from the parapet by his finger tips, his Cork backside. Collins got out of that problem, and had a word with Christy the hotel porter who came out and told her where to go in Parnell Square, and that Collins would meet her there.

When they met she told him what had happened and she said he laughed in the midst of all the stress and worry -

"God dammit, Nancy" he said, "You've heard me express my admiration of the Great Empire that could hold so many parts of the world enchained for so many centuries, and now" he said, "they are allowing all of the civilian information for Ireland to come through my second cousin!"

"From Wednesday, every day between 2:30 and 3:30 you will have whatever you decode in the hands of Joe McGrath, Liam Tobin or Desmond Fitzgerald. I want no excuses " he said. "Be there!. How you get it out - that's your worry, because when you are working for me you will express your own ingenuity and from what I know of you, you are intelligent enough, even if you are from the other side of Clonakilty". "Michael" she said, " What will I do about lunch?" He looked her up and down and said "Do without lunch and it will help to get some of that weight off you".

Joe McGrath, on left, who was later to found the Irish Hospital Sweepstakes is seen here with Michael Collins at a Pro Treaty meeting in College Green, March 1922.

The messages flowed and the war was now at its height. Collins was now under tremendous stress and one particular thing was worrying him. He met Nancy O' Brien and said to her - "Have you got any messages for me that you are not passing on?". She was carrying out the coded message in the chignon she wore on her hair. "I'm getting concerned with one or two of my colleagues who are wondering what is going on. I've given you everything I have got", she said. So he left her and five days later he came back and arranged to meet her.

"Nancy" he said, "Are you sure you are giving me everything?". "Well" she said, "apart from this very strange letter I got a few days ago supposed to be from a secret admirer. I couldn't make head nor tail of it. It referred to the seat on the canal where he and I were sitting when the Angelus bells were ringing, and the beautiful sheen of my auburn hair which caught the glint of light from the 3rd window, and all that sort of nonsense".

"Nonsense ? " he said, "The 3rd window is where Beasley and Stack are in prison, 6pm is the time of the changing of the guards and you lapped up that bloody nonsense and didn't tell me" he said. "I'm expected to fight a war with the might of Britain and my own second cousin falls for that as if it is from an admirer".

It's about time I told you that the said Nancy O' Brien is my own mother, and I have experienced occasions similar to the next minute or two when she turned around and said "I have laid my life on the line for you for the last six months and that's all you have to say to me - abuse and contempt. "You can run your own bloody war, Mick, in the future for your own Ireland. I am the leavings of the near escapes, the anxieties and all of the worries" and she stormed off and left him there.

At 2am on the following morning, at the height of the Dublin trouble and the warfare, she awoke in her digs in Iona Rd, Glasnevin to the sound of gravel being flung up at her bedroom window. She said "What a nerve. This is probably somebody that Mrs. Murphy, my landlady is to mind for a few weeks, because he is on the run from Tipperary or Limerick or somewhere like that.

She made her way to the window, and there standing in the little square of grass was Michael Collins. She put on her dressing gown and came downstairs to the hall door.

"Nancy a Gradh" he said, "Sure you're my own and you are the best I have. You've no idea of the pressures I'm under. I'm not at all well, but we must now pull off the final stroke and win. "I am in touch" he said "with my brother Johnny down at home, and the Woodfield area is where they're beginning to plan a major assault. I was anxious this evening and I'm sorry I hurt you. I was upset about it and there was no way I could go to bed without coming over to apologise to you".

This is but another example of the hundreds of incidents where Collins showed that laying his own life on the line was nothing because others were prepared to fight to the death if necessary. She was just astonished, and terrified for him having to make his way back to O'Connors by foot, - (over 4 miles to Donnybrook) during the curfew. As he headed off he looked back over his shoulder and shouted to her "Dammit Nancy, I forgot, - I left the bag of "bull's eye" sweets on the windowsill for Mrs. Murphy !".

If any of you are ever in West Cork, you should go to the place where Collins was born near Lisavaird. Stand on the foundations of the new house that my father built for my grandmother in 1900, and there in your mind's eye you can visualise the magnificent farmhouse that was there before it was burned to the ground by the British forces. Within that top room my father Johnnie, together with Tom Barry and Liam Deasy planned strategy of the Kilmichael ambush which took place on the 28th. November.

A unique picture of Liam Deasy, Tom Barry and Dan Breen, taken in 1923

Kilmichael was the catalyst in the War, with the entire force of 23 soldiers being wiped out by the West Cork Brigade.

That was the type of guerrilla warfare which was later adapted by Yitzak Shamir in the Israeli 1967 war, Mao Tse Tsung in China and the countless revolutionaries in Africa. It was the first example of guerrilla warfare brought to its fullest conclusion and that was the thinking of young Michael Collins. Shamir even called his crack regiment, "The Mickail " during that Israeli war.

One of the finest scenes in the recently released *Michael Collins* movie showed Collins' beloved henchman Joe O' Reilly coming to him on an evening of his first relaxation for years with Harry Boland and Kitty Kiernan in the Royal Marine Hotel in Dunlaoire. Kitty was dancing with Harry and Michael in the film was relaxed and nodding off as he listened to Frank Patterson's singing on the stage.

Joe O' Reilly ran in and said "Blast you Michael, I was looking for you everywhere. They're looking for a truce !". The utter sheer joy that Neeson portrayed in his brilliant characterisation of Collins summed up that one moment of precious success, - satisfaction. The joy of winning that all of us know after a lot of losses on the way up, was what Collins enjoyed to the full. Yet he was wondering what was ahead of him now. What would be the ultimate settlement?

De Valera had returned after an extraordinary seventeen months in America and Harry Boland wrote to Michael to say that his 50th attempt to see President Wilson met with the same result of the previous 49. He never succeeded in meeting the U.S. President.

There were eleven Irish - American Societies in the eleven major cites of the Sates that time. Mr. De Valera visited every one of them. He asked them to accept that they were Irishmen first and Americans second. Irish Americans, will not accept this now any more than they would accept it then.

They were Americans first for the simple reason that their parents had brought them out of an Ireland where there was no chance of work and they got that opportunity in America and to the extent that they took it they rose in American society and if they didn't take it they sunk to the depths and became ghettoised.

When he spoke to John Devoy, the greatest Fenian of them all with O'Donovan Rossa, Devoy stood before him in Seattle and said,

"No, Dev - being an American first doesn't make me any less of an Irishman, but my father brought me here after spending 12 years in British jails. I came here and I got a chance. I've made a success of my life, but that doesn't lessen my love for the homeland. It accentuates it to this extent that I now have earnings that can help".

Each of those eleven societies dissolved or became ineffective within seventeen months. Mr. de Valera came back to Ireland, and was nominated as President of the Republic by "The Blacksmith from Ballinalee", Sean MacEoin. Dev was now a man of international stature, because of the worldwide publicity given to him. In 1916 after being Comdt. in Boland's Mills he wrote claiming his right to life on the basis that he was an American citizen, and so he was saved.

DÁIL ÉIREANN

AIREACT AIRGID.

Department of Finance

TIS AN ÁRD-MAOIR,
ÁT-CLIAT

MANSION HOUSE,
DUBLIN.

3rd February, 1921.

TO:
Mr. Liam O Lorcain.

A Chara,

RE DAIL EIREANN LOAN.

    Enclosed please find receipts numbered 106321
to 106325 (inclusive) representing applications in above
amounting to £5:0:0. (FIVE POUNDS STERLING) all being
fully paid.

    With reference to second instalments - Receipts
for these are not yet being issued, but I hope to be able
to complete this matter very shortly.

Do Chara,

Micéal O Coleain
AIRE AIRGID.

Michael Collins issued a receipt for every penny of the Dáil Eireann loan. He used the above typewriter in his office in Harcourt Street for general correspondence and also for that relating to the loan.

(Left) The trap door into the attic was the escape route on the many occasions when his office was raided.

(Above left) This is a scene from a propaganda film, one of many shown in the Dublin cinemas promoting the National Loan. Here Desmond Fitzgerald makes his contribution to Collins.

Then came the Truce, and many of these simple fine Irishmen went back to their homes and pints were shoved into their hands. It was a period of great upset in Ireland. Collins saw the discipline dissolve. Breen and Tom Barry saw it and they expressed an urgency to the Irish Republican Brotherhood to get on with some type of settlement.

The first clear sign of jealousy was arising between Dev and Collins. Dev wanted Collins to go to America, and Collins knew there would be nowhere in the world he'd be more out of place. Eamon de Valera then went himself to London to see Lloyd George as to what were the outlines of the potential settlement. Over two days, he met Lloyd George alone for seven and a half hours.

Mr. de Valera was a brilliant man, a man who subsequently showed great negotiating ability and yet he knew because of his intelligence and because of the clarity with which LLoyd George put it to him that the only settlement available would incorporate in stone what was already enacted by the British Parliament, the fact that six of the Northern counties,-(though Carson looked for nine) were now part of an Ulster that wished to remain as part of the British Empire.

Eventually, a delegation was decided on to go and negotiate the Settlement. Michael Collins got the second copy of the five plenipotentiary's document and it is his copy signed by de Valera which is shown here. The document states, and note the wording; "Negotiate and conclude".

COLLINS' COPY OF PLENIPOTENTIARY DOCUMENT

TO ALL TO WHOM THESE PRESENTS COME, GREETING:

In virtue of the authority vested in me by DAIL EIREANN, I hereby appoint

Arthur Griffith, T.D., Minister for Foreign Affairs, Chairm

Michael Collins, T.D., Minister of Finance,

Robert C. Barton, T.D., Minister for Economic Affairs,

Edmund J. Duggan, T.D.,

George Gavan Duffy, T.D.

as Envoys Plenipotentiary from the Elected Government of the REPUBLIC OF IRELAND to negotiate and conclude on behalf of Ireland with the representatives of his Britannic Majesty, GEORGE V., a Treaty or Treaties of Settlement, Association and Accommodation between Ireland and the community of nations known as the British Commonwealth.

IN WITNESS WHEREOF I hereunto subscribe my name as President.

Done in the City of Dublin this 7th day of October in the year of our Lord 1921 in five identical originals.

Eamon De Valera

Collins was beginning to discern the dissensions that were beginning to build up and at first refused point blank to go. One of his closest associates was the great Bat O'Connor, whose home, lovingly looked after by Mrs. O'Connor was his favourite bolt hole. Many, many years afterwards I met her at the graveside of her husband who was buried as near to Mick as they could put him. With a smile on her 82 year old face she said ;

"Michael boy, do you know what I was saying to Bat, and I felt he understood me, even though he is buried down there 36 years?. "Bat", she said, "I don't know which of the two of you I love most, but there was nothing in it so take the odds"!.

That was the sort of relationship that was there. Their eldest daughter is now 87 and is a Carmelite Nun in Simmonscourt Road, Ballsbridge.

She tells the story that one day as a small child, she had hurt her leg the day before, and she was home from school. When Collins would call to her home she would always clean Michael's bicycle and she would get the Bulls Eye sweets from him in return. That night she heard her father and Michael discussing in an adjoining room until 5.00 in the morning. She recalls it was the only time in her life that she heard two men crying. Collins wouldn't go home.

"I'm being set up" he said, and eventually close to 5.00 am she heard her dad say, "Well everything seems to have failed, Mick, but Dev had anticipated this would happen and he asked me to ask you, to go, - for the love of Ireland?"

In his thirtieth year, Collins sat down across a table to negotiate

with the might of that British Empire. Remember that extraordinary genius that won the 1939 -'45 World War for Britain, Winston Churchill who was only the fourth in the British delegation; consisting of Lord George, Chamberlain, Birkenhead, and Churchill.

When the British Negotiators brought the signed Treaty back into the House of Commons, as one can read in Hansard, if given a chance to view it, they were castigated , demonised and absolutely abhorred by the Opposition and the general run of English people for what they gave away to this upstart Collins, and were asked how they could not brow beat "this lot of Paddies" into submission.

Years later, my father spoke with Birkenhead who told him that Chamberlain, Churchill and himself were astounded at the learning of this man, - of his knowledge of economics, of his planning for the future of his country, of the winning of the every concession, some minute, that he could get in the negotiations. That Treaty was signed on 6th. December '21 and it is absolutely true that as Birkenhead was leaving the Chamber said;

"Well Collins, I signed my political death warrant".

"That's nothing" Michael replied, "I've just signed my actual death warrant".

Collins knew the rumblings at home. I should emphasise here that every time they returned from these negotiations, Collins interceded with Dev to meet him and to discuss tactics. Dev would not have anything to do with him. Collins turned then to the Organisation into which he was sworn by Sam Maguire, The Irish Republican Brotherhood, the ultimate Organisation of responsibility. Without exception, they told Michael to do the best he could, and that no man could do more than he could.

That he did.

Collins came back to a Cabinet that was divided. Austin Stack had been promoted, though his Department, because of his inefficiency, was a joke to his colleagues. Collins felt hurt and slighted. He said to Nancy O'Brien that night, "Our Cabinet now is more divided than the Cabinet in hell. I see sad times ahead".

The Treaty terms were debated in the Chamber and the bitterness developed, but when we look at Government majorities over the world now, how many Nations would be thrilled with the majority of 2 or 3, not to mind the majority of 7 given in favour of accepting the terms of the Treaty?.

Collins begged, with all the powers he had, " Dev, now that you didn't go yourself, by all means oppose us in this House, castigate us, push us further so that we can go again, as we have the right under this Treaty to discuss it in the immediate years ahead, but, do it within the Dáil."

The treaty negotiations in London proved a difficult time for the Irish negotiating team but Collins was still able to share a joke with a colleague.

"One of the greatest things we've got" he said," is the conviction that the Boundary Commission can meet on an equal footing of two sovereign Governments. The British have undertaken that 'if three of the Six Counties wish to join the 26, then there will be no valid reason for Stormont consequently.

However jealousy and small mindedness prevailed. Collins said in those prophetic words; "It gives us freedom to achieve freedom. The ideal must always be there, and the ultimate freedom will be the determination of successive generations of Irish men and women working within the democratic process because the time for fighting is over. If we seek for that ideal, and if we come together now that we have the British Army and the British trappings of power removed, there is no limit to how far we might go".

I think History has now recorded that one of the two greatest errors committed by a great Statesman, Mr. de Valera, was in his not going to London as Head of the Treaty negotiating team. He was the educated man, being a Professor. He was President of the Republic. He was an American citizen who carried great power and had he, even after deciding not to go to London, subsequently followed the democratic process and opposed literally what the Settlement fell short of, -then democracy might have prevailed and Ireland might have gone further forward.

Mr. de Valera met the great Field Marshall Smuts. If you read Smuts' biography, you will see that he who became Governor General of South Africa after the Boer War, had come to meet Mr. de Valera, not as an emissary of Lloyd George but as an emissary of the King. He expressed to de Valera his great admiration for the work done by Collins in achieving the military freedom of Ireland.

In Smuts' biography, it states that Mr. de Valera accepted that there was no question of a Republic being attainable for generations to come.

Taoiseach Eamon de Valera with President Sean T. O'Kelly, photographed in Fethard, Co. Tipperary in the late 1950's.

The Cabinet tried to install the Treaty, which was passed by the majority itself. Mr. de Valera left the chamber and democracy was not allowed to prevail. They broke on the Oath which was an empty formula. Then came the second mistake of this man, who subsequently was a great Irish Statesman . Mr. de Valera throughout his life was a deeply conservative and religious man. He was a man of great ability and a man of deep faith. After Mass, on the 17th March 1922, he addressed a crowd of 20,000 and he said to them,

"To prevent this Treaty working, we will wade, if necessary, through brother's blood". Sadly that's what happened, and Michael Collins died in an ambush from fellow Irishmen at Beal an Blath, - one of the many tragically killed on both sides.

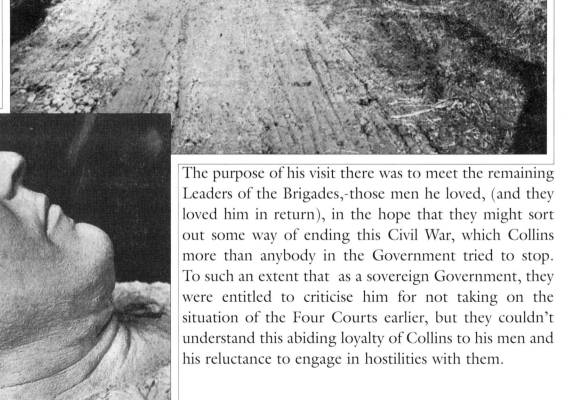

The purpose of his visit there was to meet the remaining Leaders of the Brigades,-those men he loved, (and they loved him in return), in the hope that they might sort out some way of ending this Civil War, which Collins more than anybody in the Government tried to stop. To such an extent that as a sovereign Government, they were entitled to criticise him for not taking on the situation of the Four Courts earlier, but they couldn't understand this abiding loyalty of Collins to his men and his reluctance to engage in hostilities with them.

CORK
21.8.22 @ 3.30 pm

To Mr Cosgrave

1. The Bank position here is slightly obscure. It will require a full investigation and combined with that investigation there must be an examination of the Customs & Excise position — all moneys paid in and out must come under this. We shall require three first class independent men. Unfortunately Brennan has gone to London.

2. It would be very desirable to make an examination of the destination of certain

(2)

drafts on the London County Westminster & Parrs, London Childers (Mr & Mrs) kept & keeps an account or several accounts at the Holborn (I think) Branch of this Bank. I am sure the Bank will give full details of any recent transactions.

3. I wired today to Moor Park & Kilworth — see Hogan. I told him Send down whatever man was dealing with this matter. It is urgent and we must collect back rent even though it may have already been paid to the irregulars.

3. The people here want no compromise with the irregulars

4. It is wise to postpone the Dáil meeting as already suggested.

5. You might get before your minds the three persons under Para 1, but don't announce anything until I return

6. It would be a big thing to get Civic Guards both here and in LIMERICK Civil Administration urgent everywhere in the South. The people are Splendid.

Micéal O Coileáin
21/8/22

Put superbly in that tragic five seconds in the film where the young soldier who finished off Harry Boland and said with justification that, -

"He was one of them". A broken hearted Commander-in-Chief thinking of the times that had been, said

"No, God Almighty he was one of ours". Each one of them who participated in the fight were Collins's 'till the last breath he drew.

Collins and Harry Boland in Croke Park.

continued on page 93

(On Right) Following Requiem Mass in Dublin's Pro Cathedral the coffin was placed on one of the gun carriages used in the attack on the Four Courts just a few weeks earlier.

(Below) Michael Collins lying in state from the painting by Sir John Lavery which he painted while the General's remains rested in St. Vincent's Hospital, Dublin.

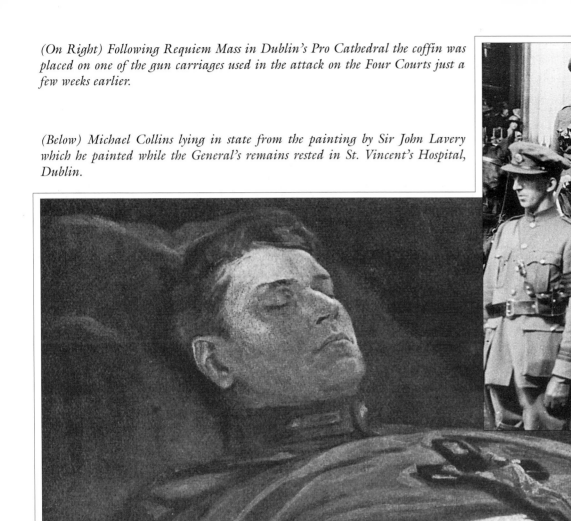

The city came to a standstill as thousands watched the cortege pass from every available vantage point.

While car loads of floral tributes followed the gun carriage, there was just one white lily placed on the coffin by Collins' fiancée Kitty Kiernan before the cortege moved off through the streets of Dublin to Glasnevin cemetery.

As the cortege wound its way through Dublin's thoroughfares it was flanked by officers and men of the newly founded Irish Army, and crowds wept openly as their hero made his final journey through streets on which he had cycled daily in troubled times.

(On Right) Among the Ministers walking behind the gun carriage were from left – Ernest Blythe, W.T. Cosgrave, P. Hogan, E. Duggan, Eoin Mac Neill, J.J. Walsh and Desmond Fitzgerald (father of Dr. Garrett Fitzgerald who was to become Taoiseach in a later government).

(Below) The cortege passes government buildings where he had done such outstanding work in his short period as Minister for Finance.

(Opposite page) The scene in Upper O'Connell Street as pictured from the top of Nelson's Pillar, one of Dublin's landmarks until it was blown up by persons unknown in 1966.

Richard Mulcahy, Emmet Dalton and J.J. O'Connell lead the Army officers in the cortege.

General Richard Mulcahy.

23.8.22

To the Men
of the Army —

3.15 am

Stand calmly by your posts.

Bend bravely and undaunted to your work

Let no cruel act of reprisal blemish your bright honour.

Every dark hour that Michael Collins met since 1916 served but to steel that bright strength of his and temper his gay bravery

You are left each, inheritors of that strength, and of that bravery

To each of you falls his unfinished work

No darkness in the hour —
No loss of comrade will daunt you at it.

Ireland the Army serves —
Strengthened by its sorrow.

Risteárd Ua Maolcatha
Chief of the General Staff

84

GENERAL RICHARD MULCAHY'S GRAVESIDE ORATION

"Our country is to-day bent under a sorrow such as it had not been bent under for many a year. Our minds are cold, empty, wordless, and without sound. But it is only our weaknesses that are bent under this great sorrow that we meet with to-day. All that is good in us, all that is strong in us, is strengthened by the memory of that great hero and that great legend who is now laid to rest.

We bend to-day over the grave of a man not more than thirty years of age, who took to himself the gospel of toil for Ireland, the gospel of working for the people of Ireland, and of sacrifice for their good, and who had made himself a hero and a legend that will stand in the pages of our history with any bright page that was ever written there.

Pages have been written by him in the hearts of our people that will never find a place in print. But we lived, some of us, with these intimate pages; and those pages that will reach history, meagre through they be, will do good to our country and will inspire us through many a dark hour. Our weaknesses cry out to us, "Michael Collins was too brave."

Michael Collins was not too brave. Every day and every hour he lived he lived it to the full extent of that bravery which God gave to him, and it is for us to be brave as he was- brave before danger, brave before those who lie, brave even to that very great bravery that our weakness complained of in him.

When we look over the pages of his diary for 22nd August, "Started 6.15a.m. Macroom to Ballineen, Bandon, Skibbereen, Roscarbery, Clonakilty," our weakness says he tried to put too much into the day. Michael Collins did not try to put too much into the day. Standing on the little mantel-piece of his office was a bronze plaque of President Roosevelt, of the United States, and the inscription on it ran, "I wish to preach, not the doctrine of ignoble ease, but the doctrine of strenuous life, the life of toil and effort, of labour and strife; to preach that highest form of success that comes, not to the man who does not shrink from danger, hardship, or bitter toil, and who, out of these, wins the splendid ultimate triumph.

Mara bhfuigheann an grainne arbhair a theidheann sa talamh bas ni bhion ann ach e fein, ach, ma gheibheann se bas, tugan se toradh mor uaidh.

Unless the grain of corn that falls into the ground dies, there is nothing but itself in it, but if it dies it gives forth great fruit. Michael Collins' passing will give us forth great fruit, and Michael Collins' dying will give us forth great fruit. Every bit of his small grain of corn died, and it died night and day during the last four or five years. We have seen him lying on a bed of sickness and struggling with infirmities, running from his bed to his work.

On Saturday, the day before he went on his last journey to Cork, he sat with me at breakfast writhing with pain from a cold all through his body, and yet he was facing his day's work for that Saturday, and

morning that I mention, he told of his visit to one of the barracks in the South on his first trip there, and of finding most of the garrison in bed at 10 o'clock; and thinking of all the lack of order, lack of cleanliness, lack of moral strength and efficiency that goes with this particular type of sloth, and of all the demoralisation following on the dissatisfaction that one has with one's self all the day that one starts with an hour's disadvantage. "Oh," he said, " if our fellows would only get up at 6 o'clock in the morning."

Yes, get up to read, to write; to think, to plan, to work, or, like Ard Riogh Eireann long ago, simply to greet the sun. The God-given long day fully felt and fully seen would bring its own work and its own construction. Let us be brave, then, and let us work.

"Prophecy," said Peter, who was the great rock, "is a light shining in the darkness till the day dawn." And surely "our great rock" was

facing his Sunday's journey and Monday's journey and his journey on Tuesday. So let us be brave, and let us not be afraid to do too much in the day. In all that great work, strenuous it was, comparatively it was intemperate, but it was the only thing that Michael Collins was intemperate in.

How often with a shout he used to get out of bed in the morning at 5 or 6 o'clock crying, "All the time that is wasted in sleep," and would dash around the room, or into some neighbouring room where some of us lay in the hope of an hour or two's sleep, and he would clear all the blankets off us, or would pound vigorously at the door which prudence had locked.

Crossing the square of the barracks on the Saturday

And just as he as a person was a light and a prophecy to us individually, he looked to it and wished that this band of brothers, which is the Army, will be a prophecy to our people. Our Army had been the people, is the people, and will be the people. Our green uniform does not make us less the people. It is a cloak of service, a curtailer of our weaknesses, and amplifier of our strength.

We are jealous for his greatness. Words have been quoted as being his last words; Michael Collins is supposed to have said the fragile words, "Forgive them." Michael Collins never said these words, "Forgive them," because his great big mind could not have entertained the obverse thought, and he knew those who sat around him and worked with him that they, too, were too big to harbour in their minds the obverse thought.

our prophet and our prophecy, a light held aloft along the road of " danger of hardship or bitter toil," And if our light is gone out it is only as the paling of a candle in the dawn of its own prophecy.

The act of his, the word of his, the look of his was day by day a prophecy to us that loose lying in us lay capabilities for toil, for bravery, for regularity, for joy in life; and slowness and in hesitancy and in weariness half yielded to, his prophecies came true in us.

When Michael Collins met difficulties, met people who obstructed him, and worked against him, he did not turn aside to blame them, but facing steadily ahead, he worked bravely forward to the goal that he intended. He had that faith in the intensity of his own work that in its development and in its construction he would absorb into one homogeneous whole in the nation, without the necessity for blame or for forgiveness, all those who differed from him and those who fought against him.

He is supposed to have said, "Let the Dublin Brigade bury me." Michael Collins knows that we will never bury him. He lies here among the men of the Dublin Brigade. Around him there lie forty-eight comrades of his from our Dublin battalions. But Michael Collins never separated the men of Dublin from the men of Kerry, nor the men of Dublin from the men of Donegal, nor the men of Donegal from the men of Cork.

His great love embraced our whole people and our whole Army, and he was as close in spirit with our men in Kerry and Donegal as he was with our men in Dublin. Yes, even those men in different districts in the country who sent us home here our dead Dublin men - we are sure he felt nothing but pity and sorrow for them for the tragic circumstances in which they find themselves, knowing that in fundamentals and in ideals they were the same.

Michael Collins had only a few minutes to live and to speak after he received his death wound, and the only word he spoke in these few moments was "Emmet". He called to the comrade alongside him, the comrade of many fights and many plans, and I am sure that he felt in calling that one name that he was calling around him the whole men of Ireland that he might speak the last word of comradeship and love.

We last looked at him in the City Hall and in the small church in Vincent's Hospital. And, studying his face with an eager gaze, we found there the same old smile that met us always in our work. And seeing it there in the first dark hour of our blow, the mind could not help travelling back to the dark storm-tossed Sea of Gallilea and the frail barque tossed upon the waters there, and the strong, calm smile of the Great Sleeper in the stern of the boat.

Tom Ashe, Tomas MacCurtain, Traolach MacSuibhne, Dick McKee, Michael O'Coileain, and all you who lie buried here, disciples of our great chief, those of us you leave behind are all, too, grain from the same handful, scattered by the hand of the Great Sower over the fruitful soil of Ireland. We, too, will bring forth our own fruit.

Men and women of Ireland, we are all mariners on the deep, bound for a port still seen only through storm and spray, sailing still on a sea full " of dangers and hardships, and bitter toil." But the Great Sleeper lies smiling in the stern of the boat, and we shall be filled with that spirit which will walk bravely upon the waters.

(Above) It was not until 1939 that the Irish Government finally allowed a monument be erected over Collins' grave in Glasnevin cemetery.
This rare photo shows however that it was well cared for in the intervening years.

The winding road, scene of the ambush at Beal na Blath, as it looked on the day the memorial to General Collins was unveiled.

President W.T. Cosgrave performed the unveiling ceremony, watched by Michael Collins' sisters and brother Johnnie.

General Richard Mulcahy later became Minister for Education in a subsequent government. He is seen here with his Fine Gael colleagues, Taoiseach John A. Costello, James Dillon and Oliver J. Flanagan pictured at the funeral of Canon John Hayes, founder of Muintir na Tire at Bansha, Co. Tipperary.

On left is another example of James O'Callaghan's outstanding photographs from these troubled times. Each day he carried to work a small fold up camera underneath his overcoat. While leaving his workplace in Broadstone he told the editor how on seeing smoke rising from the docks area on his way home he cycled in that direction and hence his capture of this unique picture of the scene after the IRA had set fire to the Revenue Commissioners records in the Customs House on 25th May, 1921.

(Above) A pall of smoke hangs over the Liffey as the Four Courts explodes.

MY UNCLE

By Michael Collins

continued from page 77

Now there was a certain cinematic licence taken in the Michael Collins movie which I have commented on both on Radio and Television concerning the blame attributed to Eamon de Valera for the actual shooting of Collins.

The facts are, the Valley of Beal na Blath lies between Crookstown and Newcestown and it is just one of these coincidences, at least I believe this, that Mr. de Valera on a visit to that part on West Cork, stayed the night prior to the ambush in Crookstown.

I believe, and truth should always prevail, that Mr. de Valera had no knowledge of that ambush. He was in that part of Cork to meet Liam Deasy, Kearney, and Kelleher, (Tom Barry was in Mountjoy at the time). Mr. de Valera had looked down the corridors of history, as he always did, and saw that the Treaty forces were inevitably winning the Civil War. Endeavoring to lessen what subsequent criticism, that might be and subsequently was levelled at him, he conspired to meet these men to see if an agreement could be concluded, but they were adamant in continuing with the fight and that they wouldn't meet him.

One of the saddest things in life is bitterness. The abiding bitterness of the Civil War was nowhere remotely felt as much between the pro and the anti Treaty people as it was felt by the anti Treaty people for the men who wouldn't see realism and carried on the fight. Their disgust and hatred was carried in many instances to their graves. The men who were pragmatic and realistic were beginning to learn, slowly, tragically what the Civil War was doing to them. This was especially so in the case of colleagues in prison, because there is nowhere better to address realistically the functioning powers of the mind, than when you are cold and hungry!. They were beginning to see that the Republic, which in their innocence they were prepared to die for and were incarcerated for could not become a reality then.

Eventually in 1927, Sean Lemass persuaded De Valera to go in to the Dail. (A generation later in 1961, I did work for the Minister for Industry and Commerce, Mr. Sean Lemass which was of vital necessity at the time. I negotiated a settlement, which if it had gone wrong would have been a matter of very serious consequence for Ireland and the Government of the day).

"Michael" he said to me, "the time for fighting was over, and the democratic process was the only way".

He said, "We were facilitated in doing that by one of the greatest and most unsung Irishman of any generation, a simple Dublin man, William T. Cosgrave".

Recently on an RTE television programme, Charlie Mc Creevy, T.D. paid a very generous tribute to that action of William T. Cosgrave's, and it was nice to see Mr. McCreevy having the guts and the decency to do it.

Think of what it might have been for this beloved country if that group, who five years later entered Dail Eireann and began the democratic process had seen fit to do so just a few years earlier. There is nothing more harmful than the Civil War in a small country. But the sadness of the Civil War was quickly followed by Mr. de Valera and his Government being able to exercise the democratic process.

Ten years after that dreadful Civil War a loyal army and a loyal police force were handed over by a very great first citizen in W.T. Cosgrave, and democracy has worked in Ireland ever since.

There are a number of personal recollections in what I have said, but it is important that you would know that during those seventeen months while Eamon de Valera was in the United States, even with the curfew at its height, Michael Collins who was "on the run" with a reward of £10,000 on his head, never failed to bring the Green Cross money to Mrs. de Valera at home in Greystones. I visited Aras An Uachtaran on the 4th and the 18th November 1966 to get and record from Mrs. De Valera her thoughts of those times.

Sinead and Eamon de Valera on their wedding day.

a daily Mass goer, always included him in her prayers. That day in November 1966 in Arus An Uachtaran she told me how when Michael Collins would come all that way out every Saturday night to their home in Greystones, he would play with each of the de Valera children for a few minutes on each visit, and they experienced great love, and childish affection from the man they called "Uncle Michael". They were heart broken when he died and not one of Mr. de Valera's children, to the last day they lived ever allowed a word to be said against the man.

Bean de Valera shortly before going to live in the Park stated

"Muna mbheadh arus beag Uí Choileain ann i bPairc na Coile in aice Cloch na Caoilte in Co. Corcaigh, ni bheadh aon Arus an Uactharain ann anois".

which translated means "Only for the little house in Woodfield, near Clonakilty in Co.Cork where Michael Collins was born there would be no Arus an Uachtaran to-day" and she went on to say "There would be no Ministers of a free Irish government in office now either without him".

Sinead Bean de Valera was opposed to the Civil War and I know for a fact that from the day Michael Collins was killed, she, who was

Included elsewhere in this book is a similar tribute from one of her grandchildren Ms. Sile de Valera T.D.

This extraordinary affection for Collins carried him through those difficult times. A lot of emphasis is given on the man as a great military genius and the fight for freedom is over emphasised at the cost of his amazing organisational ability, and his in-depth knowledge of economics which we now know about. He learned the workings of the Stock Exchange by becoming a senior clerk in a stock office. He was determined to master accountancy for the time when he would be Minister for Finance by working in the offices of Craigue-Gardiner in Dublin.

While on a tour of the military outposts in early February 1922 in Dungarvan, he was approached by an American Senator who asked him, "Mr. Collins, now that you've secured the military freedom of your country, how can you possibly survive economically? . His reply is even more relevant for his beloved country now 75 years later. "We will survive economically," he said, "if we export to the growing sophisticated markets of the world, goods of a quality which they're entitled to demand at a price beyond which they will not pay and on the day they rightly demand delivery. To meet this there is only one criteria, the pursuit of excellence".

Now as part of the EU, with Ireland being referred to as the Celtic Tiger economy, we have those services to-day, and we are exporting to the sophisticated markets of the world. Those goods and services are brought into being by countless young Irish men and women educated in their own country in the freedom of a Republic, as the old Michael Collins promised his young son back home in Woodfield, Lisavaird, would be the case one day in the future.

Many myths that masqueraded as facts about Collins have been exploded in the intervening years. He was denigrated, mis-represented, and mis-understood. Albeit belatedly, - as it is so often in life, truth ultimately prevailed and to-day General Collins strides that period of Irish history as the colossus that he was.

It is strange that this first came to light in the modern age of technology and television, where men like Robert Kee, Taylor and others were able to see through the mists the freedom which that generation of brave Irishmen had thrown up.

Collins was the man who most of all brought about the freedom of Ireland, and had he lived, I have no doubt he would have inculcated that economic endeavour with the same purposeful movement that he did while winning our freedom. He would have ensured that no more would Ireland be the fattening ground for England's cattle, because more than a revolutionary, Collins was a thinker. In the early days of the State you can look up his letters to the Dutch, the Danes and the Germans looking for their help in bringing their more up to date systems to emerging nations, such as the one he died for at the young age of 31 years.

In a recent documentary of an hour and ten minutes duration shown on French television, it finished with these closing lines. "While this young Irishman had achieved all of this at 31, General Charles de Gaule was not heard of till he was 56".

The Collins family home at Woodfield in West Cork remained as a burnt out ruin from 1922 to 1990. The old home where Michael was born had been a tin roofed cow house alongside the fine new

family home. With ruthless efficiency the young subaltern who barged in there with nine soldiers, made up of three British army, three Auxileries, and three Tans destroyed almost everything. They were brutally cruel to the family who were removed from it in under 15 minutes.

Michael and brother Johnnie inside the ruins of the family home at Woodfield which had recently been burned by the British troops in April, 1921.

I remember studying for my leaving certificate in the early 1940s. We were living in Booterstown, Co. Dublin at the time where we were almost neighbours of the de Valeras. One evening my father called up to me "Mick" he said "There's interesting news on the wireless". I went downstairs and Winston Churchhill was announcing the fall of Singapore where he said 110,000 Allied troops under Lieut. General Percival were forced to surrender to the Japanese. I listened to it with my father, mother and Peig who had come as a servant girl to my father in 1916, (being paid £6 a year with two days annual holidays.) On several occasions Peig had been offered £1,000 and a free passage to America with a guaranteed job there if she told two named local British informers when Michael was in the West Cork locality.

She sat there that night, not as a servant, but one that the 10 of us in the family loved more than we loved each other. She said to my father, "Boss, Would that Lieut General be the little snipe that gave the order that they burn Woodfield?".

"Yes Peig, it was".

"Well Boss", she said, "the mills of God grind very slow, but don't they grind fine? ".

The phone rang and I said, "Yes, General Barry he's here".

"Well tell him Mick" he said, "There's a bonfire on the ruins of Woodfield, and there's 64 pints of the Clonakilty Wrastler charged to him in the Four All's pub up at Sam's Cross". That's the way these things turned out.

On the 20th. February 1952 my father, who was then 72 years old went back to live in West Cork. A few nights before he did so, every Brigade in the 32 counties of Ireland were represented at the send-off dinner in Dublin's Gresham Hotel. It was one of the very few occasions at which General Richard Mulcahy and Mr. de Valera were ever in the same room together since the civil war. I drove him in there with a great sense of pride.

I said, "I'll head off now, but I'll be back because I want to hear you speak". When I came back, the meal was almost concluded. The head waiter came up to Liam Tobin, one of Michael's right-hand men who was Chairman for that night, and said, "The Taoiseach has informed me he has to answer questions in the Dail in 35 minutes so we had better get a move on".

Liam Tobin said, "Switch on the microphones and serve the coffee immediately, and let's get on with the speeches". My father had taken the first taste of the desert. The microphone came on and Liam Tobin's first comment was "I see you're enjoying the sweet, Johnnie", and the 350 people stopped. "By God, I am", he said. Liam continued, "I'll tell you something interesting about that sweet. The chef here in the Gresham for the past six weeks has been a chef in Buckingham Palace for 14 years". My father was taking the second spoonful, but loud and clear came the West Cork accent, "By God, Liam, I was wondering where the hell I tasted it before !".

Thank you ladies and gentlemen for the courtesy of your attention".

The Rialtas Sealadach or Provisional Government, as the name implies, was an interim arrangement which would later be replaced by the government of the Irish Free State (Saorstat Eireann).

(Above) Michael Collins leaves Dublin Castle following his taking over control of the State from the British Authorities.

Rialtas Sealadach na h'Eireann

The members of Rialtas Sealadach na h'Eireann received surrender of Dublin Castle at 1.45 p.m. to-day.

It is now in the hands of the Irish Nation.

For the next few days the functions of the existing departments of that Institution will be continued without in any way prejudicing future action.

Members of Rialtas Sealadach na h'Eireann proceed to London immediately to meet the British Cabinet Committee to arrange for the various details of handing over.

A statement will be issued by the Rialtas Sealadach na h'Eireann to - morrow in regard to its immediate intentions and policy.

For Rialtas Sealadach na h'Eireann (Signed) MICHAEL COLLINS, Chairman.

January 16, 1922

The bronze bust presented by The McGrath Family which is to be seen on the site of the Collins family home at Lisavaird.

(Right) A tribute from the man who was his friend during his early years in London.

ár laoc, ár ngiolla mear.

pádraic ó conaire do scríov.

Tuille agus deic mbliadna ficead ó soin nuair bíos féin 'mo gasúr beag óg táinic sgéala cugainn sa sgoil go raib Parnell tar éis bás d'fágáil: bí socraigte againne, páisdí sgoile, troid beit againn le céile faoi Parnell sul ar táinic sgéala a báis cugainn mar bí dream againn ar a taob agus dream eile n-a agaid, de réir baramla ár muinntire is dóca. Act nuair do cruinnigeamar le céile ar cúl an tseanpríosúin leis an gcat a tabairt, ní raid gasúr ann a buailfead a comluadar leis an mbrón bí orainn uile go léir faoi bás taoisig. Agus bíod is go raid an t-easaontas agus an droc-fuil eadrainn, do buaid an doiligeas orra. Tá taoiseac eile ar lár indiu, fear a tug saogal agus saotar ar son a tíre agus do marbuigead le piléar ó gunna Eireannaig—an mbéad sé iomarcac a ceapad go mbéad an oiread céille ag na daoine atá ag troid indiu is bí ag na gasúir d'eirig as an gcomrac bí le beit aca ar cúl an tseanpríosúin deic mbliadna ficead ó soin? Ar son na mard ar an dá taob féactar leis.   *   *   *

Suas agus anuas le ceitre bliadna déag ó soin do buail ógánac isteac cugainn i halla i Lonndain le cabrú le cúis na teangan: ní raid sé i n-aois fir act bí aoirde fir ann,—bí, agus fuinneam col na agus intinne.

WHO SHOT MICHAEL COLLINS?

By Cathal O'Shannon

Is there really any more to be written about Michael Collins? Collins had been the subject of many biographies, and countless articles in newspapers, magazines and learned journals. There has been Neil Jordan's very successful Hollywood movie, and a couple of television programmes about the Lost Leader.

It is in our nature to ponder what might have been, especially at this time. What saddens me is not the speculation on what he might have meant to this land of ours, but on the facts of his death.

Lesser men than he, often with the basest of motives, continue to ignore the evidence of those who were at Beal na mBlath. The burden of Collins' death, the guilt at cutting him down, is too much for any man to bear. It took some courage to kill him; it needed much more to admit the deed. And so men have prevaricated, lied even, not just in the County of Cork, but elsewhere.

About 20 years ago I stood on the roadway at Beal na mBlath with one of the men who was there on that August afternoon 75 years ago. The man was Emmet Dalton, a General in the Army of Ireland, and at the time Commander in the South and, as such, in charge of the small convoy of vehicles making its way back to Cork after a tour of inspection in Collins' native place. The road back to Beal na mBlath was not an easy one for Dalton. It had taken all the persuasive powers of myself and TV producer Niall McCarthy to guide his footsteps back to a place which must have been a scene of horror for him.

He was a man who was no stranger to war, of course. He had fought through the awfulness of the Battle of the Somme, and had won his MC when he was barely 19. He had then fought the British up until the time of the Truce. But nothing affected him like the death of Collins.

It is about that day at Beal na mBlath that I want to say a few things which we were unable to touch on in the film, *Emmet Dalton Remembers*. One may help to settle some of the controversy as to who killed Collins; the others are just incidents which have not been recorded until now. Dealing with Emmet Dalton at Beal na mBlath called for some delicacy on the part of those of us making the film. Our purpose was to walk him through the ambush, show us where he and Collins and the rest of the party stopped to fire on the ambushers, to identify where Collins fell, and to try to establish where the fatal shot came from.

For the first time, to my knowledge anyway, Dalton told us - on camera - that fire came not just from the hidden road which ran along the highway, but also from a small hill ahead and to the right of the convoy. We now know that these shots came from a party drawn by accident to the area by the sound of shooting while on their way home. It was, it has been established, a shot from one of these men which killed the Commander-in-Chief.

Dalton was a stern man of 80 years when we filmed him. It was obvious, however, that the experience of revisiting that awful place was an ordeal for him. He had cradled the dead Collins in his lap on that nightmare journey back to Cork city. He had covered the huge wound in Collins' head with his cap, and had arrived at his HQ with blood and brain matter on his uniform.

It was, therefore, with some trepidation that we talked later of who did what and to whom. "I know the things that people have said", he told me.

"I know that some have said that I shot The Chief. But I want to tell you, O'Shannon, that I loved that man more than anyone who knew Collins, and who knew me, knows what a lot of bloody nonsense that is."

At the time Niall McCarthy and I had been working on and off with Dalton for nearly a year. We had got to know him well. He was not prepared to discuss what he considered nonsense on camera. He would not dignify rumour or conjecture or the evil-tongued by discussing it publicly. On reflection, and as a journalist, I feel that it was a pity that he did not do so, but I must respect his reasons. His life and career had been blighted by that terrible August day.

It was painful to be asked to relive it in his old age. He did not have to justify himself.

I have no doubt at all, having spent hours, days, months with Dalton, that he was innocent of the calumnies which lesser men have uttered about that day.

Dalton was an honourable man, and few in his lifetime dared to say publicly what they have hinted at now that he is safely dead.

Two other incidents. The first concerns the possible use at Beal na mBlath by us of the armoured car, *Slievenamon*, which was in the ambush. It had been used by RTE in 1966 during the film on the 50th anniversary of the Rising. In 1977 we applied to the Department of Defence to use it in the reconstruction of the ambush at Beal na mBlath. The Department refused on the grounds that it would be "inappropriate", and no amount of argument by us could change the mind of the Civil Service.

It was an extremely odd and personal decision by one individual. However, a Very Senior Person not unconnected with the Department rang me to make a deal. He knew, he told me, two men from his own part of the country who had been among the ambushers on that day. Would I ask General Dalton if he and these two men could meet with him when we took Dalton to the ambush site?

To any journalist the chance of confronting these men with each other seemed a golden opportunity, a moment of high drama. Dalton's answer to my request was typically brusque and straightforward. He fixed me with those blue eyes of his and said: "If their only claim to fame is that they shot at me from behind a wall, I don't want to meet the bastards!" I subsequently learned that he did meet one of them, and quite amicably at that, in the old 1916-21 Club, which may no longer exist.

The second incident concerns a letter which Dalton showed me from Lady Lavery, wife of Sir John Lavery, whom Collins and Dalton had often visited in London when they were there for the Treaty talks. It was written two days after the ambush and showed a certain anxiety on the part of Hazel Lavery that some of her correspondence with Michael Collins had got into the wrong hands.

Lady Lavery was a notorious chaser of celebrities, of course, and among her intimates numbered Birkenhead and Winston Churchill - and, some say, Kevin O'Higgins.

The letter was revealing. It offered condolences to Dalton on the death of Collins and spoke of her own sorrow. She was sending the letter, she said, by Colonial Office bag, because previous letters of hers had been intercepted by Noel Lemass. She had met with Collins in Dublin on several occasions during the weeks preceding his death, and she was anxious that her husband should not know this. Would Dalton please respect her wish, she asked.

Did it mean that she and Michael Collins were more than just friends? Or was she afraid that Sir John, the complacent husband, might baulk at just one more scalp on his wife's society belt?

Countess Markievicz writes from Jail

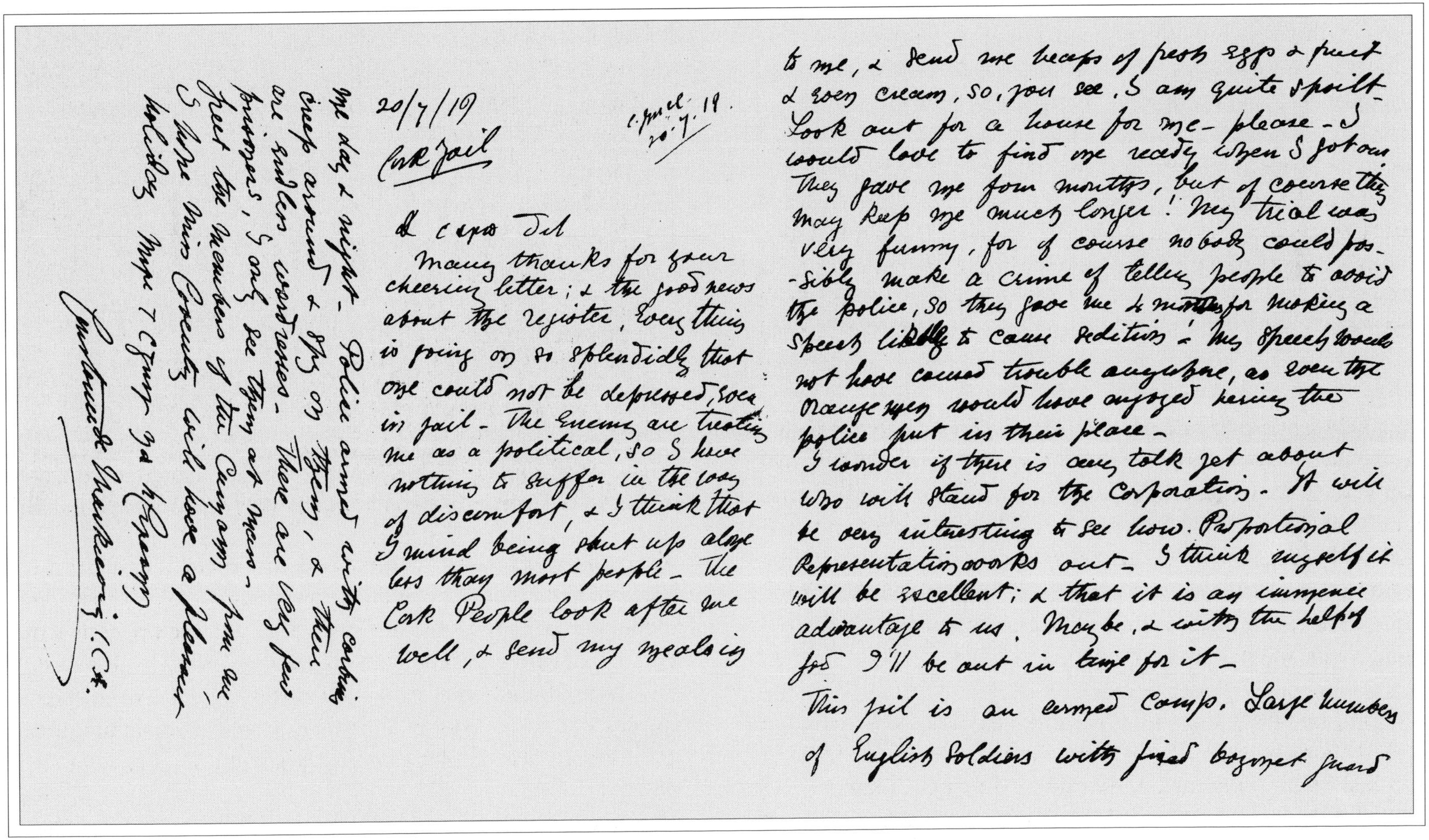

20/7/19

Cork Jail

C. Jail 20.7.19.

A cara Dil

Many thanks for your cheering letter; & the good news about the register. Everything is going on so splendidly that one could not be depressed, even in jail. The Enemy are treating me as a political, so I have nothing to suffer in the way of discomfort, & I think that I mind being shut up alone less than most people. The Cork People look after me well, & send my meals in to me, & send me heaps of fresh eggs & fruit & even cream, so, you see, I am quite spoilt. Look out for a house for me - please. I would love to find one ready when I got out. They gave me four months, but of course they may keep me much longer! My trial was very funny, for of course nobody could possibly make a crime of telling people to avoid the police, so they gave me 4 months for making a speech likely to cause sedition! My speech would not have caused trouble anywhere, as even the Orangemen would have enjoyed seeing the police put in their place.

I wonder if there is any talk yet about who will stand for the Corporation. It will be very interesting to see how Proportional Representation works out. I think myself it will be excellent; & that it is an immense advantage to us. Maybe, & with the help of God I'll be out in time for it.

This jail is an armed camp. Large numbers of English Soldiers with fixed bayonet guard me day & night. Police armed with carbines creep around & spy on them, & there are endless conferences. There are very few prisoners, I only see them at Mass. Greet the members of the Company from me. I hope Miss Coventry will have a pleasant holiday. [illegible]

Constance de Markievicz. I.C.A.

This letter although not directly concerned with the subject of the book came into the possession of the editor during his research. It is written from Cork jail by Countess Markievicz who makes interesting comments on her situation at the time.

FOLK HEROES

By Con Houlihan

Some folk heroes diminish under scrutiny - Napoleon Bonaparte is an example; some grow in stature - Michael Collins is such a one.

He has his critics; some see him as cold and ruthless, a man who shot first and shot again afterwards. In this image he is the man of action who gives little thought to the consequences of his deeds. The objective evidence does not support this image; his diaries reveal an exceptionally sensitive and intelligent man. His letters to Kitty Kiernan, it must be admitted, are sentimental to the point of childishness - but most men lose the run of themselves when in love.

Collins excelled in primary school; he had no difficulty in going from one job to another in London - and soon got employment when he moved back to Dublin. It hardly needs saying that he had an exceptionally clear mind; he exemplified Stendhal's dictum - "The hallmark of high intelligence is the absence of fuss".

He disliked politicians of all colours for a very obvious reason; words are the bricks of thought - but most politicians do not see it that way. The debate on the Treaty could be looked upon as black (or green) comedy if it didn't provide such terrible consequences. Collins commented: "To be a politician one needs to keep tongue in cheek for all of the day and most of the night, to say one thing and mean another".

The word "plenipotentiary" is deeply embedded in Irish political lore - its history illustrates Collins' comment on political language. It means, of course, one who had been entrusted with full powers - it didn't in Ireland in 1922. Collins went to London as a plenipotentiary - he had excellent reason for believing that he wasn't. Eamon de Valera and Austin Stack and Cathal Brugha refused to go; perhaps they had good reasons - but they have never been revealed.

It must be conceded, however, that Collins was ideally equipped for the mission; not only had he a clear mind - he was the Irishman most respected by the British. Lloyd George and his cabinet were well aware that he had organised the elimination of their crack intelligence corps, but they did not hold it against him. The Prime Minister's comment was pithy: "They took a soldier's chance and died a soldier's death". And that coup was probably a major factor in bringing about the truce.

The British prized themselves on the brilliance of their secret service: Collins had cracked it. Such spectacular ambushes as those at Crossbarry and Kilmichael were great sources of song and story, but it would be foolish to believe that the IRA won the war in Cork.

Tom Barry - as you would expect from one who had served in the World War - was the most successful of the guerrilla leaders, but by the summer of 1921 he was in despair. He was woefully short of arms and ammunition - and faith without good works is proverbially of no avail.

Collins tried to get a shipment from Italy - the scheme fell through. And if Barry was giving up hope, you can imagine how things were outside the County of Cork. No one, of course was more aware than Collins: he welcomed the ceasefire. That was to be seen by his critics as the high point of his career. Soon in Dail Eireann he would have to endure such words as "traitor" and being deemed worse than Castlereagh.

Time may not reveal all, but it certainly revealed the folly of those who opposed the Treaty. The Dail approved of the Treaty by a narrow margin: - the subsequent general election left no doubt about the mood of the people.

Again we are at the mercy of semantics: - the word "people" can take many meanings. Democracy was flouted in this country in 1922: that cannot be denied. The people, we were told, haven't the right to do wrong: it is a sinister dictum - and it is still at large.

The first palpable portent of civil war came when Rory O'Connor took over the Four Courts. The action placed Collins in a fearful dilemma: he was now in the proverbial no-win situation. And it was partly of his own making - or so it seems.

A bizarre deed in London in the June of 1922 may have been the catalyst of the Civil War.

The assassination of Sir Henry Wilson is surrounded by a mystery which time has not dispelled. He was the military advisor to the Northern Ireland Government: he was blamed for standing idly by when Catholics were being murdered in Belfast. As he walked home on the fateful June day, he was shot dead by two Irishmen who lived in London. One of them, Joe O'Sullivan, had lost a leg in the World War. He was a strange choice to be an assassin. The pair had no transport. Reginald Dunne was his companion in killing Wilson. They also signed their own death warrants.

As soon as O'Connor occupied the Four Courts, Lloyd George put pressure on Collins to take action. Collins did, almost certainly because he hoped to have Dunne and O'Sullivan reprieved. He told a strange story about the assassination: he said he had ordered it before the signing of the Treaty, but had forgotten to rescind the order. Few believed him. Mick wasn't a man to forget things.

One cannot help suspecting that a man who died defending the Treaty had an ambiguous attitude towards it himself. Dan Breen even claimed that Collins had asked him to assassinate Lloyd George a few months after the signing of the Treaty.

It is obvious that Collins suffered extreme mental torture in that summer of 1922. Dunne and O'Sullivan were executed on July 18; at home the mad dogs of war were at large.

The Big Fellow was in poor health. My father was a very close friend of Humphrey Murphy, CO of the Kerry No. 1 Brigade in 1920-'21. Through him he came to know Collins. He also knew some of those involved in the fateful ambush - and believed that nobody would ever know who fired the fatal shot.

Of one thing, however, we can be sure: Michael Collins' death dealt this country a blow from which it hasn't yet recovered.

Rory O'Connor, detail from a painting displayed in McKee Barracks, Dublin

IRELAND'S GREATEST IRISHMAN

By General Sean MacEoin

I first met Michael Collins in May 1917 at the South Longford by-election in which Joseph Mc Guinness was the Sinn Fein candidate opposed by Patrick McKenna of the United Irish League.

Collins had recently been released after his part in the 1916 Rising and was now secretary of the National Aid Association, an organisation promoted by friends in America, at home, and in many parts of the world on behalf of internees and dependents of people killed and wounded in 1916. The establishment of the Ulster Volunteers and the repudiation of the British Parliament showed the way for physical force.

The organised I.R.B. and Sinn Fein directed their energies towards securing the election of McGuinness. Collins, Tom Ashe and others came to the constituency. McGuinness won and we were jubilant, and I as "parish centre" of the I.R.B. invited Collins and Ashe in 1917 to visit Ballinalee and to address the people and convince them of the new policy. They came and Collins endeared himself to all of us by his affable manner and obvious leadership qualities. Ashe too endeared himself but unfortunately was arrested following his speech, and died of forcible feeding while on hunger strike in Mountjoy.

Some time later Collins addressed a similar meeting at Leggagh, in the parish of Dromard, Co. Longford. He was arrested immediately afterwards and the Crown prosecutor asked to have the case adjourned for a week but that he be kept in custody. The Registered Magistrate granted the adjournment but allowed his own bail of £50 and two sureties of £25 each. Michael Doyle of Main Street Longford and Michael Cox, Ballymahon St., Longford went as his sureties. That was the last time the British saw Collins until after the Truce. These events brought Collins very close to Co. Longford.

In 1918, Collins came to me at the forge in Ballinalee. I was very busy. He gave me the I.R.B. signal and password. He was a member of the Supreme Council and he asked me to be responsible for future operations in Co. Longford. I said I could not do it because of the promise I had given to my dying father to look after my mother and her large young family. He insisted that I must do it, and we ended up with a wrestling match to settle the matter and of course he won. From that time we were friends until his death.

I attended very many meetings and functions with him before and after my arrest in March 1921. His plans for my rescue from the British should have succeeded. His invitation to me to accompany him for his Cork, Killarney and Tralee meetings were all highlights of my life, and both his and President Griffith's attendance at my wedding was the final proof of his friendship to me and mine at a time when the Government and he were working day and night for Ireland. He was President of the Supreme Council of the I.R.B. at the Truce in July 1921 and as such was President of the Republic.

Mr. de Valera was Taoiseach and this was the very reason why Mr. de Valera wrote every day to Collins reporting his meetings with Lloyd George in July 1921. Collins being the democrat he was got the Supreme Council to transfer the Presidency to de Valera. I was instructed on 21st August 1921 to propose him and the motion was seconded by

General Mulcahy. When the Irish Cabinet appointed Cathal Brugha as Minister for Defence in September 1921 all senior officers of the Volunteers were re-commissioned to ensure that the Army would be the legal armed force of the Cabinet of the Dail.

Collins in his short life did the work of 10 men, and when President Griffith appointed him as Commander- in- Chief of the Dail forces to defend the supremacy of a democratic Dail - under the Minister for Defence, General Collins' work and responsibility were such that even his great physical strength was strained to the limit.

He was Ireland's greatest Irishman and to him we owe the freedom that we now enjoy. He died defending the authority of the elected Government of the Country. His work, his name and fame will be for the students of Ireland's History and be a shining star to guide them.

God give his gallant soul eternal rest.

General Mac Eoin with his wife on a visit to the Town Hall in Clonmel where he was granted a civic reception by Mayor Denis E. Burke, who is seen here with his wife Kitty.

"You can have all the glory, let us have all the disgrace, but let us save Ireland"

By Piaras Beaslai

AN SAORSTÁT
THE FREE STATE.
TUESDAY, AUGUST 29th, 1922.

MICHAEL COLLINS MEMORIAL NUMBER

A COMRADE'S TRIBUTE.
The Message of the Hero's Death.
By PIARAS BEASLAI.

It is seven years ago since I first met Michael Collins - then a mere boy of 25 - in the rooms of the Keating Branch of the Gaelic League, at that time situated in North Frederick Street. No inward premonition, no instinctive feeling warned me that I was making acquaintance with the most remarkable Irishman of this generation. I saw only a tall strong, good looking Irish boy, full of life and spirits, with a gay and infectious laugh, a sunny and sociable disposition, who "made friends" with me immediately.

Young as he was, Mick was already active in the Gaelic League, in Sinn Fein, in the Irish Republican Brotherhood, and in the Gaelic Athletic Association. In London he had been studying Irish, earning credit as an athlete and hurler, and concerning himself actively in the work which led up to the Insurrection of 1916. But it was first on his social and debonair side that I came to know him, and I thought of him more as a gay and pleasant companion than a future leader of the National Movement.

During the few months that immediately preceded the Insurrection of 1916, Mick spent much of his time in the rooms of the Keating Branch, which was frequented by a small group of young men who have since become famous. It is a proud thought to me that that little group were first brought together by me in an enterprise small enough in its way compared to the big national work they were destined to do afterwards. This was the formation of "Na hAisteori," a dramatic society, of which I was President, and of which the leading members were Major-General Gearoid O'Sullivan, Commandant-General Dairmuid O'Hegarty, Commandant-General Fionan Lynch, Commandant Colm O Murchadha.

When we marched behind our Commander-in-Chief at the funeral of Arthur Griffith, it gave me a strange sensation to see included in the small group of G.H.Q. officers almost all my little band of Gaelic players of 1913 to 1916. One only was parted company with us.

Mick as I said, was a constant associate of our little group. There was one other man constantly in our company whom we were proud to look on as our leader - the late Sean MacDiarmada. It was the high opinion which I saw Sean to hold of Mick Collins that first made me realise that the "Laughing Boy" from London had something more than the ordinary in him. Sean had the same capacity for inspiring love and devotion in others which Mick was afterwards to display.

The younger man loved and reverenced Sean. I have sometimes felt in after times that the mantle of Sean Mac Diarmada had fallen on Collins. With all their differences of appearance and manner, both had much in common. Their outlook was the same, their grip of practical realities, their love for the plain people, their vehement appreciation of the drolleries of humbler life in Ireland, their sociable disposition, and their power of inspiring energy and efficiency in other men.

It seems strange to think that in those fateful days, when we were feverishly preparing for the Insurrection, Mick Collins was in our midst, and was so little regarded. The man who was to lead Ireland to victory in that six years' war which we were inaugurating was then little known, little appreciated. Even our little group had not sensed the genius of the man. During the last few days before the "Rising," the rooms in North Frederick Street were an important centre of our activities. Mick was in and out continually, but was not consulted about any important matters.

On that eventful Easter Sunday, 1916, that day of orders and counter-orders, of rumours and alarms, of calling off arrangements, and calling them on, Mick was with us in the North Frederick Street rooms, gay and boyish as usual. We jested about the coming fight. In the evening Geroid O'Sullivan, Diarmuid O'Hergarty, Mick and myself slipped down town to a restaurant near the Pillar for some tea. I think it was as merry a meal as we ever had, and Mick was the life and soul of the party. We derived grim amusement from arranging with some girls of our acquaintance to go for an excursion with them on Easter Monday - knowing at the time what Easter Monday would bring.

I next saw Mick a week later a prisoner in the Gymnasium of Richmond Barracks. Detectives moved backwards and forwards among the prisoners (who were made to sit on the floor), and picked out men known to them. I was picked out and placed at the other side of the room, and found myself opposite Mick. He looked as cheerful and debonair as ever. I thought it better to show no sign of recognition, and was relieved to see that he was apparently unknown to the detectives. When the day had been spent in this weeding-out process, Mick still remained unidentified, and he was ultimately marched off with the prisoners destined for internment.

It was only after his release from internment at the end of 1916 that he began to make himself felt in the work of the nation. Even we in Lewes prison sensed, in that obscure way that an impression reaches prisoners, that Mick Collins was one of the "live wires" among the men outside. Messages reached us from him by various surreptitious channels, a system of communication was built up, and we were put in touch with the new situation in Ireland.

When we were released in 1917 we found that our boyish comrade of the previous year had become a man of weight in the work for Ireland's freedom. The Irish Volunteers were being slowly built up again after the break-up of 1916; the work had now to be done in secret, and Collins' marvellous energy and resource found employment in this work. Somehow that little group of men I have spoken of came together again - an event which seemed beyond the range of possibility on that Easter Sunday we last met. Only one man was missing - Sean Mac Diarmada - slain by the British.

We met nightly at a certain rendezvous, a place which played a big part in the history of the struggle for freedom. At a later period we had to change the rendezvous, but the habit of meeting nightly was persisted in all through the years of war that followed - even through the height of the Black-and-Tan Terror in Dublin. Sometimes one or other of the group was absent - away in goal - and when this was so, the "Big Man", as we loved to call Mick, never forgot him.

Amid the Herculean work that lay on his shoulders, amid the doubts and dangers which surrounded him, he always found time to write to "the lad in goal", to send him cigarettes, books, cheery messages, by some of the mysterious means of communication which he controlled. No other man showed more continuous and kindly thought for me during my several imprisonment's; and my experience was that of many others.

"The dearest friend to me, the kindest man, the best-conditioned and unwearied spirit in doing courtesies."

The German Plot period was the beginning of Mick's career "on the run"; it was also the period when his great work for the Army began. As Adjutant-General and Director of Organisation he did a lion's share in building up a new army from the remains of the Irish Volunteers, and at a later period, as Director of Intelligence, he made that army doubly formidable. Many mythical stories have been told of his exploits, but the true ones are amazing enough. Her is one. Early in 1919, when he was a very much "wanted" man, he actually spent a night in the headquarters of the "G" Division in Brunswick Street, then the centre of British political spy work, and acquired much valuable information.

Out little group in 1918 was reinforced by another associate - the late Harry Boland. Harry and Mick conceived a sincere affection for each other, and the unhappy political differences brought no severance of personal friendship between them. Harry, Mick, and myself being "on the run" (at that time an uncommon experience), and engaged in the same work, were constantly together up to Harry's departure for America in 1919. I am certain that no man grieved more for Harry's death under such circumstances than Mick.

It is not generally known that Mick had a warm regard for the late Cathal Brugha, which the latter never reciprocated. After the fierce attack made by Cathal on him at Dail Eireann, I remember Mick saying to me :

"Do you know, in spite of all he said against me, I still have a sneaking affection for Cathal." This was typical of the great broad-minded, broad-hearted nature of the man, free from petty malice or jealousy. A Big Man indeed!

Our little group was reinforced by some notable associates, among others Commandant General Tobin, Commandant-General Cullen, and Colonel-Commandant Frank Thornton, which last officer was recently seriously wounded in an ambush near Kilkenny. These three were Mick's chief intelligence officers, and no team ever gave more loyal, brave, and magnificent service. The day has not yet come when the full story of the work done by those men and the group of brave men who served under them can be fully told; but it was admitted by the British military authorities during the recent war that the effectiveness of the I.R.A. Intelligence Department was simply marvellous.

The nightly meetings of our group were a combination of social intercourse and business. I believe that they were an important factor in the effectiveness of the work. At the chosen rendezvous Mick met his Lieutenants, met heads of other Army Departments, met officers from the country, and kept in close touch with them all. As we had to operate in different furtive offices scattered all over the city, this nightly personal intercourse was of immense personal importance.

During the height of the Terror, when the British Army and Auxiliaries were combing out Dublin for Michael Collins, there never was a night that a crowd of very much "wanted" officers did not meet their beloved Chief at the same rendezvous. His vital energy was never more strikingly displayed than on these occasions. Everybody had business with him; everybody called him aside to discuss some problem or give him some information.

He concentrated his mind on each new question with startling rapidity, came to a rapid decision, made a brief note, and passed on to something else. You could be sure the matter noted would not be forgotten. He was the man who remembered and got things done. Then business done, he would relax, begin to jest or even to indulge in horseplay with all the zest of a schoolboy.

He was much addicted to practical jokes. At this time, when a huge price was on his head, with lorries thundering by in the streets outside our place of rendezvous, he was ever the gayest of the gay, full of exuberant animal spirits, and our meetings were as merry as if no dangers surrounded us.

His many miraculous escapes gave him, I think, and gave us all a kind of blind confidence in his luck. Let there be no mistake about it, his many escapes were due to sheer luck, courage, and confidence, and not to any special "elusiveness," disguises or mystery. No wanted man ever took less precautions. He never wore a disguise, and always went anywhere business called him, even the most prominent places in Dublin. His only precaution was to ride a bicycle, and not to sleep for many nights in succession at the same house. Again and again he was held up and searched.

On one occasion, Christmas Eve, 1920, he, in company with Commandant-General Tobin, Commandant-General O'Connell, and Rory O'Connor of "Four Courts" fame, was actually captured by Auxiliaries in the Gresham Hotel, but after an hour's detention and interrogation they succeeded in bluffing the "Auxies," as we call them, into releasing them.

The legend of Mick's "bodyguard" of armed men who always attended him seems hard to kill. I can state in the most emphatic manner that there is no truth in it. All through the blackest days of the Terror, Mick moved freely about on his bicycle without any guard or companion. The legend of the "bodyguard" was invented by the British Intelligence Department to explain their failure to capture him. In similar strain in the present troubles, the organ of the Irregulars described Mick as moving around Dublin "in an armoured car". At the time in question I had met the Commander-in-Chief riding through Dublin in full uniform in an open touring car containing only himself and the driver.

I have often been struck by the resemblance in character between Danton and Michael Collins. Both had the same intense love of their country, of the plain people of their land; the same vital energy in a moment of national crisis, the same fiery spirit, the same large, generous nature, Like Danton, Collins saved his country, and fell because he disdained to take precautions. Danton uttered one of the greatest phrases in history: "Let my name perish, but let France be saved." Collins at the secret debate on the Treaty said something similar in an appeal for an arrangement in Ireland's interest. "You can have all the glory, let us have all the disgrace, but let us save Ireland."

I have been permitted by a friend of Mick's and mine - one of the little group who met together in the times of storm and stress - to make use of two private letters received by him from "The Big Man" only a few days before his tragic end. These letters, not intended for publication, contain some phrases which show the outlook of our lost leader on the present situation - his sanity, his big, broad, generous statesmanlike mind, in the midst of a crisis when smaller men lose their heads at the spectacle of wanton destruction.

He said:- "Anybody who is out for blood or scalps is of little use to the country; equally, of course, the real issue cannot be departed from .... I for one will always be found on the side of any arrangement that will give the country the chance it desires and will safeguard the future."

Again, in the second letter, he says:- "If people had a little truer appreciation of other people's opinion, we might never have got into this present morass."

Michael Collins is gone. A week before he died I marched behind him at the funeral of Arthur Griffith. I heard that mass of splendid manhood blessed and prayed for by the people along the route as the hope of Ireland, I saw him gazing on the grave of his colleague, and thought what a heavy weight had descended on those strong young shoulders. To-day the strong form is powerless, the gay laugh is silenced. A career of brilliant promise is ended in the very beginning of its usefulness. But that inspiration which he gave to those who loved and followed him will not die, and those who are left will not desist from their efforts till Ireland has attained that peace and freedom for which she longs.

This group of government ministers, led by W.T. Cosgrave, is pictured during the funeral of President Arthur Griffith as the cortege moves up Westland Row.

Eamon de Valera and colleagues at the funeral of Joe McGuinness T.D.

DEV AND COLLINS WERE "GOOD PALS"

By Sile de Valera T.D.

MICHAEL COLLINS is one of those names in modern Irish History that elicits an immediate response.

Whether it be positive or negative, the response is definitive. Although I grew up in what is nowadays termed a different political tradition, the name Michael Collins was always spoken with respect and affection. In this context, I was encouraged to seek out the personality of the man, and how it helped to shape events. With this approach I felt I came to know something of the person, his qualities, his strengths, his failures.

There seems to be an approach at present by revisionists to harp on a limited number of qualities concerning the decisions Michael Collins made during the last years of his life. While these questions can be interesting, if examined in the full context of the period, revisionists have attempted to explain his actions by distorting the events that took place between 1920 and 1922 and, in so doing, have also distorted the image of the man himself.

Rather than concentrating on the purely political and military elements of Michael Collins' life, I would prefer to attempt to try to bring together the different aspects of his character which I have read about over the years, and any information I have gleaned from those who knew the man personally.

Sinead de Valera, while differing with him on his stance on the Treaty, had a great friendship for the man throughout the Civil War, and she remained friends with members of the Collins family until her death.

Mr. Liam Collins once told me of his fond memories of happy afternoons in her company. Such a lasting friendship is not surprising when you realise the sad, difficult and indeed dangerous times up until 1921 that were shared between Michael Collins and the de Valera family.

It was Michael Collins who ensured Dev's safety, time and time again, by arranging safe houses, false passports and playing a significant part in arranging Dev's escape from Lincoln Jail. Such life experiences bind people together and such bonds are not easily broken.

Eamonn de Valera would never criticise his old comrades in arms who found themselves fighting opposite him in the Civil War. de Valera looked on Collins as someone who had given so much service to the Irish cause and had shown so much personal loyalty to him. He liked to recall both he and Collins as having been "good pals". Eamonn de Valera recognised in Collins a splendid revolutionary leader and an excellent executive, someone who could get to the heart of the matter and get things done.

Michael Collins was a tall, handsome figure who was quick to laugh or cry. Although his lifestyle meant that he had to be a tough, uncompromising military leader he showed moments of great compassion. He shed tears on hearing of Kevin Barry's execution by hanging and showed similar reactions on hearing of the deaths of Boland and Brugha, although the latter and Collins had very fundamental disagreements in the last few years of their lives.

Collins could be extremely impatient and would not suffer fools gladly. For him time was of the essence, and he would not tolerate tardiness. There is one well known incident where a messenger was six minutes late meeting him, and was greeted with some sharp and uncompromising words!

Collins was immensely proud of his rather pronounced Cork accent, a quality which was my aunt Maureen's outstanding memory of him.

It is said that his natural understanding of, and empathy with, old people grew from the fact that his father was in his seventies when Michael was born. This strength, or quality, does not always manifest itself in someone so young.

Michael Collins also had great time for children. Ruairi de Valera recalled an incident where Collins, Dev and Harry Boland, had been out for the day in County Wicklow attending to some target practice. They were all discussing how well Dev hit the target (a Bovril packet!). He was considered a good shot. That night as they had visitors, the children were allowed to stay up longer than usual. Then came the time for young Ruairi to retire, but Michael Collins put in a plea for him, saying: –

"Only bad boys go to bed early"!.

During the time when Collins was on the run he thoroughly enjoyed defying the authorities by openly cycling around Dublin. He could safely do this as there was only one photograph of him in the authorities' possession, and so he was not immediately recognisable. This part as the Scarlet Pimpernel really suited his mischievous sense of humour!

What is it about this proud, jovial Corkman that keeps attracting attention? An interest in him can become a fascination and, for some, a preoccupation. What is it about this man that, although one may hold the opposite political viewpoint and differ with him on the most fundamental of policies, one still feels a great liking and deep respect for him?

Perhaps it is because Collins, a humourous, clever and witty young man with such potential, died at the age of 31. Perhaps it is because

Members of the government and Pro-Treaty members of Dáil Eireann in February, 1922. Collins is seated fourth from left in front row.

he was seen to be a glamorous and romantic figure; perhaps because of the sad figure of Kitty Kiernan, his fiancee, left behind. All these can be the ingredients of myth. However, I believe the reason is more basic.

Although Collins was said by some to be impetuous and susceptible to flattery, he had an underlying honesty and principle - an honourable way of dealing with others which made it possible to admire and respect him while at the same time differing on fundamental matters.

Coupled with this principled approach, Collins was a man of physical and moral courage. These were the qualities which, in my view, brought the prisoners on the opposite side to him in the Civil War to their knees in prayer in Kilmainham Jail on hearing of his death. Surely such a spontaneous reaction was the greatest tribute that could be paid to the man they knew as "The Big Fellow".

Even in those days the candidates had to travel through their constituency when an election was in the offing. For Collins however it was a labour of love when he toured his native county.

THE BRAVE DIE YOUNG

By Diarmuid Fawsett

The brave, as the good, die young. In the case of Michael Collins it is but too true, he was brave and young, brave to the point of rashness; young in the mind as in years. It was his bravery and his youth that won our hearts and our sympathies, long before we awoke to his other and more enduring qualities, his selflessness and his statesmanship.

Peace! His great soul abhorred the very thought of civil war in Ireland. A war between the people to be fought out by brother Irishmen, to have ranged with him and against him those loved comrades of the dark yet glorious period, 1916 - 1921, to slay and to be slain by his own, and on the threshold of National Victory!. This was to invite back the British, to complete our nation subjection and economic disintegration. This thought was ever present to his mind and so civil war between Orange and Green or between brother Irishmen was something to be avoided as leprous and deadly.

Only at length, when all his moves for peace had been misused and ultimately rejected, and when war was thrust upon him, did he grasp the sword in defence of the rights and liberties of his people. Only those of his intimates who knew him can realise the terrible ordeal of mind he suffered when the final decision had to be made - a decision which demanded faith and courage and self-effacement.

To find himself opposed in arms to Harry Boland, to Cathal Brugha, to Eamonn de Valera, to Tom Hales, - those loved comrades of earlier days! He was loyal Irishman enough to make the decision - as he was courageous and wise enough to efface his open feelings and to sign a Treaty of Peace with England that ensured to Ireland a recognition of national status and a restoration of national authority that had been withheld from our country for a week of centuries.

Peace! In those latter days he knew that he was a "marked man", and he told this to a "peace" agent from the county in which his great soul was born and was finally extinguished just a few days before his death. To another he wrote two days before his killing, "Let them all come – we should be able to stand up to such gentlemen (assassins) as we did to others of the same persuasion for the past two or three years."

And he went on with his life's work - he waged war to win peace for his country and to restore those dearly-won rights and liberties that he had offered up his young life's every endeavour to achieve for the plain people of Ireland.

The brave - as the good - die young! His death has left a void in our political life that cannot be filled. But even in his death he as left us all an example of generosity, of service, of love that should steel us to crown his living triumphs. He was good, he was wise, he was brave, he was young! Let us resolve to raise to his memory and indestructible cairn - a freedom-loving people in a free, peaceful, and prosperous Ireland.

SOUVENIR ALBUM

Pen & Picture Record of the Revolt against the Treaty

Photo by Panograph Co.

A Full Story of the Battles Exclusive Views and Portraits

OF THE DUBLIN FIGHTING, 1922

Printed and Published by The Brunswick Press, Ltd., Dublin

PRICE ONE SHILLING

A FAMOUS BATTLE GROUND

General view of the ruins in Upper O'Connell Street after the fighting and fires.   To the right are the remains of the Hammam Hotel, then come the Accountant's Office, G.P.O.; the General Post Office, the Granville Hotel and the Gresham Hotel (also in ruins).   The other end of this well-known thoroughfare (Lower O'Connell Street), it will be remembered, was destroyed during the 1916 Rebellion.

[Photo by Keogh Bros.

Ruins of the Granville Hotel and the General Post Office. It was here that the last stand was made by the Irregulars.

[Photo by C. & L. Walsh.

Firemen at work on the Dublin United Tramway Co.'s offices at the corner of Cathedral Street.

THE birth of the Irish Free State has not been without sore travail. The roar of cannon, the rattle of machine guns, and the noise of other arms, accompanied by the still more dreaded sound of burning, have combined to usher in the new order of government laid down in the terms of the famous Treaty, which, signed by the British and Irish representatives on December 6th, 1921, was ratified by Dail Eireann a month later, and ultimately confirmed by the majority vote of the Irish people. The Revolt of the summer of 1922 differed in its nature from all previous risings in Ireland from the fact that it was not now an outside force that had to be engaged, but one section of Irishmen was in opposition to another section of Irishmen, men fighting men of the same birth and blood, brother ranged against brother. The root cause of this latest and most regrettable (as it must be to all classes of Irish men and women) chapter in the history of the nation is to be traced back to the first memorable Dail sittings, when the Treaty terms were considered and ratified. In opposing this agreement, Mr. De Valera found a certain amount of backing, not only in the Dail Assembly, but also in the ranks of the Irish Republican Army, of which he was then the head; and the inevitable consequence was a splitting of the latter force, the Free State adherents becoming the recognised regular National Army, and the others breaking away and setting up under separate control, with headquarters ultimately established at the Four Courts (Dublin), of which they had taken forcible possession. During the subsequent months the raiding of private premises and the plundering of private property became of frequent occurrence throughout the country, while a stringent boycott was declared against Belfast goods, but it was not until the end of June, seven months after the signing of the Treaty, that any serious conflict between the two armies occurred. The events leading directly to the first acts of war are interesting and worth recording in detail.

Events Leading Up to the Fight.

On Saturday, 24th June, two Dublin firms received demands in the name of a leader of the Irregulars in the Law Courts to pay certain sums of money by the following Tuesday. The Government, on receiving information of the attempted extortion, arranged to have any persons attempting it arrested if and when they proceeded to enforce their demand. On the following Monday afternoon a raid was attempted on the premises of Messrs. Harry Ferguson & Co., motor engineers, Baggot Street, Dublin, by Mr. Leo Henderson, described as Director of Boycott, by instructions issued to him from the Republican Headquarters at the Four Courts. While this raid was in progress a party of National troops of the 1st Eastern Division, Wellington Barracks, arrived on the scene, " held up " the raiders, and arrested Mr. Leo Henderson. Later on the same evening Lieutenant-General O'Connell, Assistant Chief of Staff of the National Army, who had been in Dublin for the week-end on Army business, was seized, while proceeding in uniform, and unarmed, from a friend's house in Leeson Street to Beggar's Bush Barracks, and taken as a hostage to the Four Courts pending the release of Mr. Henderson and of some other men who had been arrested in Drogheda while searching a train for Belfast goods. Thus was performed the opening act in a drama that was to develop so rapidly and with such tragic effect.

Government Proclamation.

The next day, Tuesday, 27th June, the following public statement was issued by the Provisional Government:—

" Since the close of the General Election, at which the will of the people of Ireland was ascertained, further grave acts against the security of person and property have been committed in Dublin and in some other parts of Ireland by persons pretending to act with authority.

" It is the duty of the Government, to which the people have entrusted their defence and the conduct of their affairs, to protect and secure all law-respecting citizens without distinction, and that duty the Government will resolutely perform.

" Yesterday one of the principal garages in the metropolis was raided and plundered under the pretext of a Belfast boycott. No such boycott has any legal existence, and, if it had, it could not authorise or condone the action of irresponsible persons in seizing private property.

" Later in the same evening Lieutenant-General O'Connell, Assistant Chief of Staff, was seized by some of the persons responsible for the plundering of the garage, and is still held in their hands. Outrages such as these against the nation and the Government must cease at once, and cease for ever.

" For some months past all classes of business in Ireland have suffered severely through the feeling of insecurity engendered by reckless and wicked acts, which have tarnished the reputation of Ireland abroad.

FOLLOWING THE FIGHTERS—continued.

As one disastrous consequence, unemployment and distress are prevalent in the country, at a time when, but for such acts, Ireland would be humming with prosperity.

"The Government is determined that the country shall no longer be held up from the pursuit of its normal life and the re-establishment of its free national institutions. It calls, therefore, on the citizens to co-operate actively with it in the measures it is taking to ensure the public safety and to secure Ireland for the Irish people."

The First Shot.

Actions quickly followed words. Early on Wednesday morning parties of National troops were on the streets, stopping vehicles and pedestrians and searching them for arms. At the same time much activity was manifested at the Four Courts, where works of defence were being erected in the shape of barbed wire barricades, etc. The first shots were heard about 4 a.m., and shortly after it became known that an attack by the National forces had begun on the Four Courts and on the Orange Hall and adjoining Fowler Memorial Hall, Parnell Square, which were also in the hands of the Irregulars. Before opening fire, however, Commandant Ennis, who was in charge of the National troops which had surrounded the Four Courts, sent an ultimatum to the occupants demanding the evacuation of the building and the surrender of the munitions and property which they held. A time limit was given, but the demand was ignored. In conducting their attack the National troops brought into action both machine guns and field guns, in addition to small arms, and the noise of firing was heard intermittently throughout the day, much to the alarm of the citizens who crowded the principal streets and sought anxiously for news. To add to the excitement several ambushes of the National troops occurred in different parts of the city. The most serious of these took place at Leeson Street Bridge in the early afternoon. While driving towards Donnybrook in a motor car Staff-Captain Vaughan, Col.-Comdt. Mandeville, and three soldiers, all attached to Beggar's Bush Barracks, were fired on by a group of men standing on the bridge. Capt. Vaughan was severely wounded in the back, and succumbed in Vincent's Hospital. Col.-Comdt. Mandeville sustained severe wounds in the left side

and legs, which also proved fatal; while two of the soldiers were wounded in the feet and thighs. Another fatal affray occurred in Upper Abbey Street, where a Crossley tender containing National troops was also fired on. The soldiers in this case escaped, but a young man standing near by was shot dead. Later in the evening a young girl was mortally wounded during an ambush of troops in Harcourt Street, while another girl was seriously injured. Many other casualties resulted from ambushes during the day, over twenty cases being received at the different city hospitals.

Irregulars' Strongholds.

Snipers were also active in many parts of the city, and several business premises and hotels were reported to have been seized and barricaded by the Irregulars. Meanwhile the attacks on the two central positions of the Irregular forces were heavily sustained. In the case of the Orange and Fowler Halls the continuous fire of machine guns and rifles soon made itself felt, and shortly after noon the premises were abandoned, the occupants leaving by the back entrance. By this time a fire had broken out which threatened the total destruction of the buildings, but by the efforts of the Fire Brigade the flames were successfully got under, though not before the ground floor portion had been completely destroyed. In launching their attack against the Four Courts the National troops first surrounded the block of buildings and occupied every post of advantage in houses and on roofs overlooking the Courts. Armoured lorries and machine guns were placed in every commanding position, while on the opposite side of the river, facing the Four Courts, was an 18-pounder gun, mounted on an armoured car. The occupants of the Four Courts, under cover of armoured plates and other powerful works of defence, at once gave reply to the fire of the attackers, and as the day advanced the exchanges became more and more intense. The deafening noise of the battle was heard throughout the whole city and suburbs, and the vibrations from the big shells as they crashed against the masonry of the Four Courts were felt at a considerable distance. The effect of this was to strike terror into the hearts of those whose homes lay within near distance of the battle zone, and many families had to leave their homes, while the numerous guests in the neighbour-

ing hotels had also to pack up and get out. As night drew on the firing became less intense, but about midnight, or in the early hours of Thursday, a fresh outburst occurred, the citizens, or those of them who had succeeded in getting to sleep, being specially startled by one terrific explosion which virtually shook the city to its foundations. This was understood to have been caused by the discharge of one of the big guns at the Four Courts.

Address to the Troops.

Throughout the ordeals of this, the first day of fighting, the National Army displayed wonderful coolness and bravery, which was only equalled by the daring and stubbornness of the Irregular forces. In a stirring message to the troops, Mr. R. O. Maolchatha, Minister of Defence, said: "To-day, having driven the tyranny of the stranger from our land, instead of having the opportunity to turn to these services of construction, which must develop and crown the strength of our country, you are called upon to serve her still in arms, to protect her from a madness from within, from men who seek to inflict injury and injustice upon particular individuals, and upon particular sections of their countrymen, and who conceive the mad purpose of driving our country by such actions back into a war which can be avoided for her; and by taunt and threat and forced disorder drive our gallant people hopelessly into a struggle that their strength cannot stand. In Dublin some of you find yourselves to-day ranged in fighting against some who have been your comrades. The fundamental reason is that they systematically challenge 'the rights and liberties common to all the people of Ireland,' the security and maintenance of which have been the aim of your arms since 1913. Only in pursuance of a clear and stern duty could we hope to surmount the ties of comradeship and affection that bind us to those against whom we find ourselves ranged. No scrap of effort that these ties might have has been spared to endeavour to avoid such a conflict. Let us remember that comradeship and that affection as a true strength to us while we stand firmly by our duties of to-day with a steadfastness not less than that of yesterday."

A quiet morning on Thursday was followed by still more desperate fighting, and over a more widely extended area, as parties of armed Irregulars had by this time established themselves in many pre-

The Four Courts before the Fight.

The Four Courts after the Fight.

[Photo by Keogh Bros.

Damage caused by shell fire to East Wing of Four Courts.

[Photo Lafayette.

View of the Solicitors' Hall, Four Courts, one of the many splendid apartments destroyed by the explosion and fire.

Inside views of the ruined Four Courts, showing the ornamental pillars in the Central Hall and damaged statues of Rt. Hon. Michael O'Loughlen, Bart., Master of the Rolls (left), and Lord Chancellor O'Hagan (right).

[Photos Lafayette.

[Photo by C. & L. Walsh.

GROUP OF HEADQUARTERS' STAFF OF NATIONAL ARMY.
Front row—Mr. R. Mulcahy   Gen. E. O'Duffy   Lieut.-Genl. O'Connell   Comdt. Ennis.
(Minister of Defence).   (Chief of Staff).   (Asst.-Chief of Staff).

The printing blocks of all the pictures appearing in this Album have been made by the Irish Photo Engraving Co., 50 Middle Abbey St., Dublin

[Photo by C. & L. Walsh.

COMDT. LEONARD AND BRIG.-GEN. O'DALY,
Who led the attack against the Four Courts, the former being slightly wounded.

[Photo by C. & L. Walsh.

GROUP OF THE DUBLIN GUARDS AT BEGGAR'S BUSH BARRACKS.
This regiment distinguished itself at the final attack on the Irregulars' stronghold in O'Connell Street.

FOLLOWING THE FIGHTERS—continued.

mises in the centre of the city. The business life of the city came to a standstill, shops and offices closed up, and, except for the bravely curious, the citizens beat a hasty retreat to their homes. Barricades were also erected across the main thoroughfares and strongly guarded by National troops, and pedestrians as they passed were subject to a careful, but courteous, search. Snipers became increasingly active to-day, operating from roofs and windows, and many more ambushes of the National troops took place. The bombardment of the Four Courts continued from early morning with occasional short intervals, the boom of the big guns again being accompanied by the rattle of machine guns and rifle fire. Still heavier guns were now being used by the attacking force, and their effect became apparent by the weakening response of the besieged party. The great building itself was also showing the worse of the onslaught; the entrance gates had long since been smashed in by the shell fire, gaping holes were torn in the massive walls, while part of one of the wings was seen to be blown completely away. The dome above the central hall was shot away.

Fall of the Four Courts.

It was not, however, until the afternoon of Friday, June 30th, that the chief citadel of the Irregulars was surrendered. The building was first stormed by the National troops, who succeeded in dislodging the Irregulars from the greater part of the buildings. This was carried out under heavy fire from within, and during the storming Commandant J. Leonard was wounded, but not seriously. Comdt. McGuinness and Comdt. T. O'Connor broke through the Church Street side and effected an entrance to the Courts without suffering any casualties. By midnight on Thursday the National forces had occupied the greater part of the main building, including the Central Hall and the Library, and the Irregulars were forced to retire to the rear, being confined in the east part of the rear building, a considerable portion of which had been blown away. Thirty-three Irregulars were taken prisoners. The story of the final surrender was described in the following words in the official bulletin issued from G.H.Q.:—

"The Four Courts, the headquarters of the Irregulars, was surrendered to the National forces at about 3.30 p.m. to-day. The troops in occupation of the Central Hall and the main building continued to press the attack from early this morning, forcing the Irregulars to retreat further to the rear of the building. At 11.30 a.m. a fire broke out in one of the wings, but this did not interfere to any extent with our troops, who remained in the front buildings. At 12.30 p.m. the retreating Irregulars exploded a ground mine under the Central Hall, in which fifty of our troops were stationed. All the men were injured, thirty being seriously wounded. The leader of the Irregulars admitted after the surrender that the mine was deliberately exploded by them, and expressed surprise that the troops had not suffered greater casualties. The fire continued to spread, necessitating the withdrawal of our troops to the streets about 3 o'clock. At 2.30 p.m. all firing by us had ceased. The Irregulars left the building at 3.30 p.m., their leader surrendering unconditionally on behalf of his followers to Brigadier-General O'Daly. The prisoners, who numbered about 140, were marched to Jameson's Distillery, Bow Street, and later removed under a strong escort to Mountjoy Prison. They included Messrs. Rory O'Connor, Liam Mellowes, Joseph McKelvey, A. Doyle, Sean MacBride, etc. In all, 170 prisoners had been taken. During the course of the operations three of our troops were killed and five officers and fifty rank and file wounded. The casualties among the Irregulars were comparatively slight."

It was also learned, with relief, that Lieut.-General O'Connell, Assistant Chief of Staff, who had been held a prisoner in the Four Courts, had been set at liberty, and was none the worse for his terrible experience. The explosion of the mine referred to above caused a tremendous sensation in the city, and its effects were felt in houses two miles away. Several large plate-glass windows in the centre of the city was shattered by the concussion. Valuable documents and papers which had been stored in the Four Courts were flung high into the air and fell half-burnt on all parts of the city, while the dense volumes of smoke that poured from the scene of the explosion betrayed the fact that the famous Courts had taken fire. The Fire Brigade gallantly rushed to the scene, but what with barbed wire, barricades, falling masonry, and the danger of further mines, nothing could be done to save the historic pile, which by this time was a roaring furnace, and the efforts of the firemen could only be directed to saving the adjoining buildings.

Scene of Attack Transferred.

The fall of the Irregular headquarters did not, however, mean that the final defeat of the Irregulars had come, for desperate fighting was at this time being waged in other parts of the city, principally in a wide area just north of Nelson's Pillar. The forces that had been driven out of the Fowler Hall on the previous day had joined their comrades in establishing themselves in various buildings in O'Connell Street, Marlborough Street, Gardiner Street, Talbot Street, and other parts. Amongst the premises seized were Moran's Hotel, Barry's Hotel, Messrs. Eason's, Arnott's, and the Rutland High School, and from these points of 'vantage the Irregulars kept up a fire upon the National troops throughout Friday and the following day.

A strong position was secured by the Irregulars in the Rutland High School, a large building which stands on a commanding position at the corner of Rutland Square and Granby Row. This was seized on Wednesday afternoon by a party of fifty or sixty men, who at once proceeded to barricade doors and windows. The effect of this investment on the resident girl pupils can better be imagined than described, but Principal Anderson, with the aid of other teachers, managed to get their charges safely out of the building and away. The armed men continued in possession of the school for several days, but fortunately—for the building—no attack was made by the National troops, and eventually on Monday, July 3rd, the Irregulars decided to abandon the premises. Amongst the articles left behind by the invaders was the following typewritten document:—

Saturday, 1st of July 1922. Time—Midnight.

"During the past 24 hours we have extended our battle line, which now covers an area embracing the northern portion of Parnell Square. Our activities during that time have been mainly directed towards fortifying and manning our extended positions; while doing that we have been able to harass enemy troops by sniping tactics. Our position is now stronger than ever. We await the coming attack with steady hearts and strong right arms, confident that when it comes we will once more prove to the enemy we are determined to stand to the last man in defence of mother Ireland."

MR. ARTHUR GRIFFITH.

GENERAL COLLINS.
[Photos Lafayette.

LIEUT.-GENERAL O'CONNELL.

COMMANDANT ENNIS.
[Photos C. & L. Walsh.

Leaders on the National Side

Mr. Arthur Griffith is President of Dail Eireann. He was the founder of Sinn Fein, and has been the foremost figure in the movement since its inception. One of the original signatories of the Treaty, he spoke powerfully in its defence at the subsequent meetings of Dail Eireann, and since the setting up of the Provisional Government he has proved himself a wise leader and able statesman.

Mr. Michael Collins, or General Collins, as he is now to be called, shares with Mr. Griffith the chief responsibilities in shaping the destiny of the new Irish Free State. Though his name is now a household word, Mr. Collins first came into prominence during the 1916 Rebellion, in which he proved himself a clever and daring fighter. When the new Government was formed Mr. Collins was appointed Minister of Finance, a position he has now relinquished to take up the still more important duties of Commander-in-Chief in the War Council, which has been created by the Government to direct the military operations now in progress.

Lieutenant-General O'Connell is Assistant Chief of Staff in the National Army. His arrest by a party of the Irregulars on June 26th, and subsequent detention at the Four Courts, were the direct cause of the recent fighting. The story of how he was seized while walking along a Dublin street, and how eventually he was liberated after a thrilling experience in the Irregulars' chief stronghold, is told on another page.

Commandant Ennis was one of the most prominent figures on the National side in the Dublin fighting. He it was who first led the attack against the Irregulars' headquarters at the Four Courts, and who helped to sustain the onslaught until the final fall of the enemy's citadel.

Leaders on the Irregulars' Side

Mr. Eamonn de Valera, at one time head of the Irish Republican Army, has been a bitter opponent of the Treaty from the start, and when his followers actively set themselves to withstand the lawful claims of Government he definitely sided with them, and was reported to have actually taken up arms against the National troops. His peaceful calling was Professor of Mathematics, and he recently received the honour of being appointed Chancellor of the National University.

Mr. Rory O'Connor, son of a Dublin solicitor, acted as chief leader of the Irregular forces operating in Dublin, and was one of the besieged party in the Four Courts. After the final assault by the National Army, and when his stronghold had taken fire he surrendered, with some 140 of his followers, to Brigadier-General O'Daly, and was removed under a strong escort to Mountjoy Prison.

Mr. Cathal Brugha, another of the Irregular leaders, who, however, rather than surrender, gave his life in a last desperate effort to escape from one of the burning buildings in O'Connell Street, where the last concerted stand of the Irregulars was made. He was born in Dublin forty-five years ago, educated at Belvedere College, and became a director of the firm of Lalor & Co., Dublin. A strong Republican in his views, he also took a prominent part in the Rebellion in 1916, when he was severely wounded.

Mr. Liam Mellowes was also first publicly noticed in connection with the 1916 Rebellion. He was then in command of the Irish Volunteers in Galway, and succeeded in making his escape to America. On returning to Ireland he became a strong supporter of Mr. de Valera, and when the Revolt broke out was amongst those who sought to hold the Four Courts against the National Army. He surrendered along with Mr. Rory O'Connor, and was lodged in Mountjoy Prison.

MR. EAMONN DE VALERA.

MR. RORY O'CONNOR.
[Photo Lafayette.

MR. CATHAL BRUGHA.
[Photo by Lafayette.

MR. LIAM MELLOWES.
[Photo Keogh Bros.

View of the Gresham, one of Dublin's finest hotels, just before the walls collapsed.

[Photo Lafayette.

Interior view of the Gresham Hotel before the Revolt, showing the grand staircase.

[Photo Lafayette.

The handsomely furnished ladies' sitting room of the Gresham Hotel, which, with the rest of the building suffered complete destruction.

[Photo by Keogh Bros.

All that now remains of the Gresham.

FOLLOWING THE FIGHTERS—continued.

Hemmed In!

The fighting continued on and off all day on Sunday. The official report issued on this evening stated:—" National forces are now carrying out a big concerted movement round the O'Connell Street area, which is the stronghold of the Irregulars. From early this evening they have been closing in and drawing a cordon round O'Connell Street, Marlborough Street, and Gardiner Street. The troops advanced from three different directions, and have penetrated as far inwards as the north end of Lower O'Connell Street, occupying in their advance the La Scala Theatre, Arnott's, Henry Street, and Todd Burns. The Irregulars were driven out of Arnott's. On the north-west side the National forces occupied positions about Parnell Street and Dominick Street, with posts at King's Inns Street, Granby Row, and the corner of North Frederick Street and Dorset Street. The houses 13 and 14 Lower Dominick Street, commanding the rear of Parnell Square, West, were also taken by National forces, and the Irregulars driven out, some of them being captured and made prisoners. A further advance in the Parnell Square area is being made. The National troops operating in Amiens Street have occupied the premises of Duggan (chemist), at the corner of Summerhill and North Circular Road, and are advancing towards Mountjoy Square. From the railway bridge corner of Talbot Street they attacked the Irregular posts at Brooks Thomas; MacArthur's, Moran's Hotel, Hughes's Hotel, and the Holyhead Hotel. Machine gun and rifle fire only were used in the attack."

During these operations, which were carried out by the Dublin Guards, several ground mines that had been laid by the Irregulars were exploded, including one laid at Moran's Hotel, Talbot Street, and another laid under the railway bridge crossing the same street, but they did no material damage to the bridge. A little later the National troops succeeded in capturing Moran's Hotel, Hughes's Hotel, and MacArthur's, and making some prisoners. By this evening it was estimated that the Irregular forces had altogether lost in captures and casualties about 450 men.

The Attack on O'Connell Street.

By the morning of Monday, July 4th, the fighting zone had become limited chiefly to the Lower O'Connell Street area, and the citizens began to venture out a little more, though business premises, for the most part, still remained closed. Snipers were still active in various parts of the city, north and south, but no serious engagements occurred outside the above-mentioned area, which was now surrounded by National troops. A fresh attack on the occupied premises in O'Connell Street was launched on Monday afternoon, the heavy guns again being brought into play here. Further successes quickly followed for the National arms, several of the remaining positions held by the Irregulars being captured, including the Gresham Hotel and the Y.M.C.A. premises opposite, and it was officially reported that a large number of prisoners were secured, many of whom were trying to get away with their arms and ammunition. Unfortunately fire broke out shortly afterwards in the large premises of the Y.M.C.A., and, ere the Fire Brigade could arrive, had obtained such a hold that all hope of saving the building was abandoned.

Despite these reverses, the Irregulars continued to show resistance, and all Monday night and Tuesday morning held out defiantly. Early in the Tuesday afternoon, however, further defeat overtook them, a white flag being displayed from a window of the Hammam Hotel, to be followed by the surrender of about twenty Irregulars. These came out by the rere, having been forced by the deadly concentration of the National troops. An 18-pounder gun had by this time been placed at the corner of Henry Street, from which position the Hammam Hotel and adjoining premises were shelled. Tuesday night and Wednesday morning still found the garrison of the Irregulars holding out, though it was apparent they could do so but little longer. A fierce bombardment had been maintained throughout the night, and several of the buildings on the east side of O'Connell Street had sustained heavy damage as a result of shell fire.

The Last Stand and Surrender.

Some time about noon on this day, Wednesday, July 5th, saw the beginning of the end. A fire broke out in the neighbourhood of the Hammam Hotel and another building. The flames spread quickly from the ground floor to the upper storeys of both premises, and a dense volume of smoke mounted skywards. There were frequent explosions within both buildings, whose fronts were blown away. Soon both premises were a mass of flames, and as they burned a fierce fusilade of machine guns was directed against the Gresham Hotel. The fire spread quickly to the Hammam Hotel, where tongues of flames were emitted. The upper portion was soon enveloped, and loose ammunition exploded at intervals with a crackling noise. The firing continued with increased force, and amid the din the Fire Brigade, in charge of Captain Myers, dashed up intrepidly to try and subdue the outbreak, which by this time seemed to have involved the entire buildings. Soon after the arrival of the firemen the front walls of the Hammam collapsed with a loud crash, accompanied by blinding volumes of dense black smoke. Simultaneously there was a further crash from Messrs. Moore's and Gleeson's premises. Undaunted by the magnitude of its task, the Fire Brigade got to work strenuously, and its efforts were mainly directed to preventing the fire from spreading in a northern direction, while attention was also paid to the Bible Society's building and the Tramways Company's offices. A terrific explosion was next heard near the Gresham Hotel, and it was followed by a deafening roar of machine guns. The Gresham Hotel was still standing, but, later on, it, too, became involved and was quickly a mass of flames. The efforts of the Fire Brigade to save it were fruitless, and the handsome structure was soon beyond redemption.

The last building to come under fire was the Granville Hotel. It was stated that Mr. Cathal Brugha, with a few followers, including Mr. Austin Stack, had taken their final stand there. The fire was now raging furiously, and it was seen that the back of the Post Office and the chemical stores which extend under the Granville Hotel had become ignited. In these circumstances the place soon became quite untenable. The roof by this time had fallen, and immediately after calls of surrender were shouted from the building. The white flag was also displayed, and at 7.30 p.m. the Irregulars, to the number of about twenty and led by Mr. Art O'Connor, marched out and surrendered. The party included four women, one of whom was Nurse Linda Kearns, head of the Irregulars' nursing department.

LT.-GEN. FINIAN LYNCH.

[Photos Lafayette.
MAJOR-GEN. McGRATH,

COMDT.-GEN. O'HEGARTY.

[Photos C. & L. Walsh.
COL.-COMDT. O'HIGGINS,

Who have been appointed to co-operate with the new War Council, consisting of Generals Collins, Mulcahy, and O'Duffy, in directing the military operations.

[By courtesy "Irish Life."
Mr. R. Mulcahy, Minister of Defence; Lieut.-Genl. O'Connell, and Comdt. Ennis watching the march past of the National troops at Beggar's Bush Barracks.

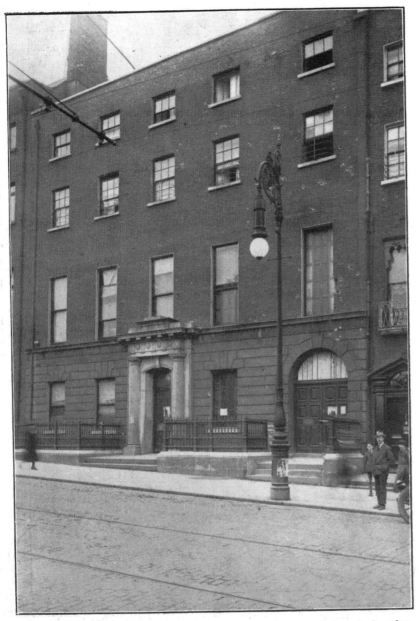

[Photos C. & L. Walsh.

View of the Orange Hall and Fowler Memorial Hall, Rutland Square, out of which the Irregulars were driven. The latter building was considerably damaged by fire.

The residential quarters of the Rutland High School for girls, which was also seized and barricaded by the Irregulars.

Another view of the destroyed premises in Upper O'Connell Street, looking north from the corner of Henry Street.

[Photo by Keogh Bros.

[Photo by Panograph Co.

Party of Irregular prisoners made by National Army in Dublin being marched away to prison.

[Photo by Panograph Co.

Passengers to and from the city were subject to a careful search for arms.

FOLLOWING THE FIGHTERS—continued.

Leader's Last Desperate Effort.

There was still one man missing, Cathal Brugha, the last of the Irregular leaders. He did come out eventually, not, however, to surrender, but to make a last desperate bid for freedom. It was a most dramatic scene, and is best described in the following words of an eye-witness:—

" 'Where's Brugha?' shouts someone. 'God help us, he's burned, he must be, he wouldn't come along with us.' A Red Cross nurse began to cry aloud. A man on a pallet wounded in the forearm became hysterical, began to shout, 'Only 10 of us, you only got 10 of us.' On the right sleeve of his torn overcoat a cloth with a red cross upon it was tied. 'No, no, no,' said St. John's men, bending over him. 'Don't say anything; remember your Red Cross.' He tried to vociferate, half got up, staggered. They put him down gently. 'But where's Brugha?' rang the cry again. I ran out, tried to make a way out past the barricade, for loud cries were coming from there, but the flames beat me back. They were almost across the lane, the barricade was blazing, smoke from the cataclysm of falling buildings came drifting over us, snipers were still shooting somewhere, soldiers coming up. There was the white flag. In the midst of the lane a man was standing, a man in civilian clothes, filthy with dust and powder and everything. He was a heavily built man, with a heavy, determined face—Art O'Connor, whom I had last seen in the Dail on the bench behind De Valera and Childers. Defeated at the elections, he was now in the atmosphere that suited him best. The flames came out with a rush. We got into the garage (at rere of Granville Hotel). Everyone seemed to be there, doctors, firemen, soldiers, and a handful more of the men in civilian clothes, grimy with dust and powder, everything that in a beleaguered house falls upon the besieged. They were mostly young, pale-looking, strained, and wan. Their dirty overcoats were bespread with sacred badges. Most stood silent. There were 10 of them we were to see presently when they lined up. But one or two spoke wildly, incessantly. 'Where did you keep to the end?' I asked. 'We stood it. We didn't give in till the fire was all around us.' 'But where?' I shouted. 'Sixteen of us, and five went this morning.' You couldn't get a coherent answer from him. But it was in the red outbuilding they

had been. The outhouse was surrounded with flames when Brugha finally came out. He leapt through the flames into the lane, revolver in hand, singed, panting. A doctor and a St. John's man rushed at him. 'Stop, stop,' they cried. 'No, no,' he yelled, and, revolver in hand, went rushing up the lane at the soldiers there. Picture this and the flames and smoke and all the shouting and cries. They were obliged to bring him down. A shot was fired from the building at the lane end. Brugha fell with a broken leg, shot through the thigh, in a circle of blood. I think he had lost consciousness, for, as they lifted him in, rapidly bandaged, he gave no glance at any of us. The pale, angry, determined face lay back flat and motionless upon the stretcher."

He was conveyed at once to the Mater Misericordiae Hospital, where an operation revealed the fact that, in addition to a broken thigh, one of the principal arteries and the sciatic nerve were severed. Some slight hope was entertained of his recovery, but on the following night (Thursday) a change for the worse set in, and at 10.45 on Friday morning Cathal Brugha breathed his last.

Conclusion.

Thus ended a week of terror and destruction that is equalled only by the Rebellion of Easter, 1916. The loss of lives in the case of the military totalled 19 dead and 122 wounded, and of civilians over 50 dead and 200 wounded. The value of the destroyed property, which included some twenty of the finest buildings in the city, is estimated at between three and four million pounds, while, besides the many ruined homes, the damage has resulted in the disemployment of several hundred men and women. As regards the combatants, both sides may be said to have fought with magnificent bravery— the one with unflinching obedience and

discipline, the other with that reckless daring that befits a desperate cause. The splendid service rendered by the doctors, nurses, and Red Cross men, many of whom hazarded their lives in attending to the wounded, was beyond all praise, and no less a tribute is to be paid to the gallant members of the Dublin Fire Brigade, who readily answered every call, and, oftimes in the midst of flying bullets, sought to quell the flames.

It cannot be said the last shot has yet been fired. Spasmodic firing is still to be heard within the city boundary. But the Revolt has definitely been broken, and, so far as general life in the Capital is concerned, the bullet-scarred buildings and smouldering ruins alone remain to remind us of the nightmare that has passed.

[Photo by Panograph Co.

Press photographers and cinema operator watching the fight in O'Connell Street.

EPILOGUE
By Justin Nelson

Most Irish families have some story to tell about the Civil War. Growing up in the 1940s on the Sligo-Leitrim border, I can recall the clearly divided loyalties within our parish, which was typical of rural Ireland at that time. However, I have no idea which political persuasion my own parents professed, because my father being the local school teacher was careful to remain neutral, and as a result the Civil War was never mentioned in the history class in our National School at that time.

Another reason for his obvious neutrality was his role as Presiding Officer for each general election, and I recall the excitement of being with him as a small boy on such occasions. The two main political parties would each have engaged a "hackney" car for the entire day in order to ferry the older parishioners out to vote. At the close of polling, each party's tallyman would accurately foretell the parish outcome of the election by simply noting the numbers from each family in the parish who had turned up to vote, – so divided were the family loyalties as a result of the Civil War.

Going back a further generation, I have in my possession an ornate gold medallion which my mother gave me before her death.

Presented to her brother in 1913 by the Michael Davitt Branch of the United Irish League in Wigan, *"For services to the Cause"*, I can only imagine how he would have fared during the 1919 – 22 period if the great flu epidemic had not snuffed out both his own and his brother's lives within a week of each other.

Having come home from England they had set up a Grocery and Provisions business in Sligo town, and many RIC Barracks are listed as regular customers in their shop ledgers which I still have.

As happened all over the country, the local barracks at Fivemilebourne was attacked and burned down by the I.R.A. I have a copy of the diary extract from the I.R.A. Staff Sergeant involved in the ambush which sounds like it was a "Dad's Army" type operation!

It reads as follows;
"Attack June 1920 – arms used were – Sligo Company, revolvers and hand grenades – Grange party – rifles and shotguns. For some weeks we filled the grenades with gelignite and detonators and bottles with petrol to burn the barracks – we went out twice to view the ground – on the night of attack we left the club at 10.30, went across the gardens of Abbey Street, up Cairns, across the lake (Lough Gill) by boat, 9 or 10 of us – imagine our plight when it stuck on a rock – but landed safely at Hazelwood, went to the 'Bourne by back road.

"B.P. went up on the roof to break a hole in it and throw in a large grenade – he fell down and that finished that. He then threw a grenade in a window, but it failed to explode – after a bit of firing we called off the attack and started the tramp back and row across the lake. It was 9 a.m. before I got home. After this, the R.I.C. left the barracks and we went out and burned it."

I don't imagine Michael Collins would have given them a high rating for their efficiency! The resulting burnt out shell, (see photo) was later purchased by my father which he rebuilt in 1926 and it was here I first saw the light of day a decade later.

My great interest in photography from childhood ensured I would spend my entire working life to date in a visual medium. In the late 1950's, while working with *The Nationalist* in Clonmel, I photographed many of the leading personalities who took part in the War of Independence – men like; Eamon de Valera, General Richard Mulcahy, Sean T. O'Kelly, General Sean Mac Eoin, Dan Breen and others involved in the Soloheadbeg Ambush.

Later, during more than 30 years as a TV Producer in various Departments with RTE, I was assigned to the TV coverage of many general elections in the '70s and 80s, but somehow they never held the same fascination for me as those boyhood elections when I would play with the long wooden baton carried by "Big Pat" Flynn, the Garda sent out from Sligo town to keep law and order during the day's polling in my father's National school!